Oh Da Joy

"*Oh Da Joy* is a joy to read. It asks the right questions and gets us thinking about how we bring joy to our lives and to others. Pat encourages us to live in the moment. Thinking about what might and could happen steals our joy. She cautions, "What one expects is what one finds most of the time." Every chapter ends with a thought provoking message.

"Joy comes in being happy with being you, but without needing to make others be you," is imperative to living a life full of joy. We're all different and that's okay. Celebrate that in you and in others.

Will there be days when joy may not lighten your life? Yes, but in those days, there will also be moments when it will. We have to *seek* joy. We have to *create* joy. We have to *want* joy. We have to *be* joy.

Everyone will benefit from *Oh Da Joy*. The stories allow us all to know that joy can happen in our lives, though we may not always feel joyful, we can live every day in joy, finding it in everything we do."

- Montrie Rucker Adams, author, *Just Do Your Dream! Seven Steps to Help You Do What You Always Wanted*

***

"Pat Jewell is an extraordinary teacher not only in her classroom but in life. She shows compassion, empathy, and love in some of the most challenging situations in her amazing way by sharing her stories. She take you on a journey of how we as humans behave and react in life. You will relate, learn and grow as she continue to teach you to find your own joy in life."

- **Kathy Buckley; America's first hearing-impaired comedienne, author of "*If You Could Hear What I See*", Inspirational Speaker. She has been on the Tonight Show, Good Morning America, and many others. Her latest video on her Facebook has had over 34 million hits.**

***

"The advice in this book is so good that I'm going to ask Pat Jewell to be my therapist."

- **Chip Beall; CEO and Founder of *Questions Unlimited* and the *National Academic Association***

Oh Da Joy

A CONVERSATION IN THE ART OF JOYFUL LIVING

Pat Jewell

KHARIS PUBLISHING

Published by KHARIS PUBLISHING, imprint of
KHARIS MEDIA LLC

Cover artwork by Dennis Vargo

ISBN-13: 978-1-946277-39-8
ISBN-10: 1-946277-39-8
Library of Congress Control Number:2019948931

All KHARIS PUBLISHING products are available at special
quantity discounts for bulk purchase for sales promotions,
premiums, fund-raising, and educational needs. For details, write:

Kharis Media LLC
Tel: 1-479-903 8160
support@kharispublishing.com
www.kharispublishing.com

TABLE OF CONTENTS

Introduction

There was a curve in the road on the way to my son's house — a sharp right angle curve. On the railing that kept people from flying into the back yards ahead was a sign: NO OUTLET. I began to chuckle, as I often do when I wonder at the why of things. Of course there was no outlet — there was no road. So why the sign?

Someone thought it through, I'm sure. Maybe someone had flown into one of the backyards on the other side of the railing at one time. I don't know. They had a reason that is just incomprehensible to me with my limited knowledge. Then again, I'm probably not the one to ask for the reasons. I tend to think…backwards from many people. That is likely the most apt description. I always have. I didn't realize it at first in life, but then I thought there must be something wrong with me that I was always looking at things from a different angle than most. I can't be blamed for this fallacy, for the depth of understanding of who I am had not yet sunk in. I am actually now extremely grateful for who I am, for it has brought me to live my life in Joy. There isn't a thing wrong with thinking differently and seeing a unique perspective. I am exactly who I've needed to be for what I do in life. I'm not expecting anyone to come away from this book seeing my perspective; I'm hoping that people can find new ways to add Joy to their lives from their own viewpoint.

I've learned not to always share those little chuckles of mine. There are those who don't find the signs and silly little things of life that delight me to be very humorous. Some moments have even brought the chuckles to peals of laughter when people are puzzled by the giggles when they begin to bubble up. Some of you are definitely not laughing now.

How can I hold back the Joy? It's not that I don't see the hard things around me – they can neither be missed nor dismissed. They cannot obliterate all of the good either. I hope perhaps in sharing the Joy of life to bring a smile to others as well—even if they are laughing at me instead of with me. At least they have been able to discover something that makes them wonder what on earth someone is thinking and to be able to find some humor in their day.

When I'm done with the little bursts of giggles, I start to really ponder what those little things that have caught my attention can tell me about life. It's not really an abrupt change of pace—it's the reality that small life lessons can come out of the most obscure places. For me, they come as questions needing answers and the relating of details to the bigger picture.

I laugh at the NO OUTLET sign. I wouldn't try to drive down a road that obviously doesn't exist. Would I? Yet I'm not sure that it's true in life sometimes. My stubbornness can lead me to try to make roads where they don't exist simply because it's what I wanted to do. It hasn't always turned out well and the crumpled bumpers of my wrecked pride have been the result. There are times when I do need the warnings. The sign reminds me of this lesson: I should stop and listen, and think before I set out trying to take a path I've created on my own. There are times when I should and do make my own path, but that's a different lesson.

In these pages, are some of those laughs and some of those crashes and some of the lessons found along the way. May they bring you chuckles and help you find ways to bring more Joy into your life.

• LIFE LESSON 1 •

What Were You Expecting?

I t was my third year of teaching and I was working with an absolutely incredible school, teaching gifted elementary students in North College Hill, Ohio—just north of Cincinnati. It was really tough to find out mid-year that I would be moving to North Carolina at the end of the school year. When you teach a multi-age program, you look forward to working with the students for years, and this was heart-wrenching. The students were wonderful, and their parents were incredibly supportive. We all just worked together. It was a dream job.

We planned a huge end-of-year picnic at a local park the day after school let out – time to enjoy together before saying farewell. We were all so excited, expectant…

The deluge that we woke up to that morning was frightening. It wasn't one of those little drizzles that will blow over with a little patience. It was one of those "can't count the lightning strikes, swim down the road" storms that will take over the day. The parents and I agreed with a couple of phone calls to cancel the event.

I lay on the floor of my packed-up living room and cried my heart out. I wanted the time, the laughter, the Joy, the time to say good-bye. I expected it.

I was disappointed.

I moved a couple of days later and never had the chance to say those goodbyes.

There are times when we know exactly what we expect of life. We plan it all out, we think it through, we make decisions based upon those expectations.

Life doesn't always work that way.

There's not a thing I could have done about the rain. Storms come in life. That's how life is. It doesn't care that it dashed my expectations.

I did not respond to it in Joy. My sorrow overwhelmed me. I can't tell you that in the years since 1982 that I've never responded to disappointment with sorrow. Don't we all sometimes? So, how do we get to the Joy here?

First let's digress a little.

I'm one of those people who think that the glass is half-full – actually, I'm closer to thinking that it's really, really full. I expect the best at all times. Half-empty people tell me that they are less disappointed when bad things happen because they are expecting it. The old optimist/pessimist variance.

People do tend to look at things differently, don't they? Most will agree that neither person is really wrong. Just coming at things from another lens on life. So this is not a condemnation on those who are more pessimistic.

Those who are always believing the worst often say that they are not pessimists, that they are realists. Assuming that bad things will happen, they consider ahead of time what to do and prepare for it. On those occasions when they are correct in the assumption, they are ready for it and know how to respond. They are not disappointed for they've expected it.

I understand the logic behind this, but let me ask you something before we get to the other side of this approach.

What do you expect from life?

Life is filled with ups and downs. The worst imaginable sorrows and overwhelming Joy. Serious hatred and incredible, heart-filling love. Fear and peace. Triumphs and tragedies. Living has heart-breakers and heart-fillers. Some lives have more of one than the other, but life has both.

So whichever I expect, it will happen. At least sometimes. And sometimes I'll be surprised by the worst case scenario. Just as others are surprised by the good things.

So, if both sides are surprised by some of life's experiences, why even consider the questions?

The answer is that, if one expects the best, one can live life joyfully anticipating and enjoying what is happening at the time. I don't want to spend any of my time worrying about things that haven't happened—and may not. Worrying about filling the half-empty glass keeps me from drinking the water that is there this moment. I'll refill when needed (or half refill), but for now let me drink of life. Let me enjoy the sunrise without assuming that bad things will happen during the day. Let me kiss my husband goodbye as we head off for work without assuming that something bad will happen to one of us that day. Let me head to work appreciating the beauty of the leaves gently falling to the ground without fearing winter. Let me go to work and find Joy in the smile of a coworker as we greet each other. Let me love my work as I see students enjoy learning and want to know more without fearing that the job market will crash around me tomorrow. Let me enjoy evening talks with my family members and friends and walks through the neighborhood. Let me view the glories of the sunset without fear of the night. Let me enjoy the night air and the beauty of the countless stars above. Let me plan for the best with the coming sunrise and the new day tomorrow. Let me savor all the best that life has to offer.

The logical among us may say, "But you have to be ready…" and it is absolutely true that one should have basic plans in case anything does go wrong. Planning financially for one's future, keeping one's home in the best repair possible, planning details for work, and transportation, and family care—those things in life we need to take care—these are essential. That's different than spending time assuming the worst in all cases is just right around the corner, about to happen, crouching like an attacking lion waiting to consume us. Get ready, put aside the worry, and enjoy the good happening at this moment.

When that storm happened, I was surprised and disappointed. But it wasn't something I could have prevented. It was just something that happened in life that I couldn't deal with until it happened. I cried and let out my frustration – and moved on ready to believe that most of life is not disappointing and hurtful.

What one expects is what one finds most of the time.

If you were to keep a chart and honestly put it on the good things in each day on one side and the bad things from that day on the other side, what would you see mostly?

I recently helped pass groceries out to people who lived at a senior citizen apartment complex. One woman came up in a small motorized chair to receive hers. We introduced ourselves and chatted a little and she said something very profound to me. Her statement was, "We can never count our blessings—for there are far too many. I may be in this chair, but I cannot count my blessings. We can count our tragedies, for they are far fewer." I was amazed and realized that she was right. I have had tragedies in my life—but the number is so far less than all of the wonderful things in my life.

Yet, when we are anticipating the worst, it seems to be all that we see. We say, "See, I told you that would happen and it's worse than I thought." We could be saying, "This is awful, I wasn't expecting it, but I will get through this and I will be alright." I'd rather live in Joy and be surprised with occasional pain than living in worry and being surprised by small glimpses of Joy.

I don't believe that shifting one's point of view is an easy thing. That sure hasn't always been true for me. However, if one wants to be joyful – and I'm hoping that after reading this far you want to be, then sometimes there has to be a conscious decision to focus on the positives of life instead of the negatives. It may take actually making that chart and working to find the best around you. It may take asking your more positive family members, friends, coworkers, and acquaintances to help you find something positive and good around you. It takes refocusing.

It also takes an understanding that people sometimes look to the worst even if they are optimists. Humans can get down sometimes. Life can get to us, and our own thoughts and worries can get to us. That's when we have to decide whether to continue to focus on the worst, or try to find the best.

A.A. Milne wrote all the fun stories of Winnie the Pooh and his friends a long time ago. Milne understood the different approaches people take to life.

You have Tigger happily bouncing around on his tail, and you have Eeyore always expecting that nothing good will happen. Christopher Robin is there for them both no matter what. Tigger could use a little understanding that you can't just bounce around in life without seeing some issues you don't know how to handle, and Eeyore needs to see that he is loved and that the worst doesn't always happen.

Somewhere in between the Tiggers and the Eeyores of this life are the people who know how to plan for, and handle, the difficult parts but who can enjoy the best life has to offer most of the time.

Rarely do I ever purchase a refrigerator magnet, but I recently got one that spoke to me. It says: *Life isn't about waiting for the storms to pass. It's about learning how to dance in the rain.* I'm still learning to dance sometimes but what a happy dance it can be.

Expect the best and let your Joy shine through when it happens every day.

• LIFE LESSON 2 •

Don't Be Me and I Won't Be You

I was an adult when I found out that I tie my shoes backwards—a complete mirror image from most. I don't know how I hadn't realized it sooner but I guess I don't keenly watch most people tie their shoes. I found out when someone saw me tying my shoes and asked why I did it backwards. I wonder why I was surprised at the question. I do lots of things backwards. I do long division short and upside down. Often, I start magazines from the back. I've been known to go to the end of books and see if I like the ending before getting very far in—and yes, I quit reading if I don't like the ending.

I shouldn't have been surprised. I pondered the question and thought about how I learned to tie my shoes. I remember it very clearly: my grandma faced me and had me put my toes against her toes. Then, she had me replicate each movement. Make the loop, go around the loop, push through. We did this several times and I had it! I was so excited—I could tie my shoes! Of course, it was backwards.

Once discovered, though, the question is what does it really mean? There are many things in life that we do because it's the way we've learned it or taught ourselves. We think that they are being done the way they should be done. "This is the way to do this." Then we go off to college, or get married, or move out with roommates, or join the service, or whatever takes us away from our cocoon where we have gotten ready and matured before taking our wings and flying. Wait, why does that roommate hang the toilet paper with the paper going down the back? Don't they know if hangs down the front? Why are they upset by my soaking the pan in the sink to get the stuff off of it easier instead of washing it immediately?

How much of the interpersonal agony of this world results from us believing that our way is THE WAY? I don't have an answer to that question beyond the obvious—it's a lot. We lost all sense of individuality in the process. Be yourself, but do it like me. Strange and impossible dichotomy, yet it resonates within us. Why? I believe it's because it injures our egos to believe that maybe we aren't doing something correctly. We defend ourselves by insisting that people do everything exactly the way we do it.

Joy comes in not having to ask others to be us. It comes because we start to realize that for some things in life there is no real "right" way, therefore, I'm not wrong and neither are you. We respect ourselves and others best by deciding that the differences are interesting and fun, not horrible causes for judgment and argument.

This does not relate to facts. I cannot decide for example that the Earth is five times the size of the sun and ask you to believe me. My students cannot tell me that they have decided that $22 + 6 = 4000$. It simply isn't true. Sometimes those facts are vital to share – and sometimes not. Hint: if you wouldn't want to be corrected on a fact of who was in what movie, in what year, in front of lots of people at dinner, they probably won't want to be either.

This is where some might start saying, "Perhaps I should throw this book out. It's getting controversial." I hope you'll be open-minded and hear me out. This concept also doesn't apply to beliefs in the purest sense, in that there have been belief systems throughout history that have been proven inaccurate. The Mayan calendar notwithstanding—the world did not end in December of 2012. They never said it would when they stopped making calendars, but many believed it anyway. Greek and Roman mythology is called MYTHology for a reason. I may or may not decide that I can wash out that pan right away rather than soak it because there really isn't a "wrong" or "right" way to take care of the situation any more than there is a right way to tie my shoes. However, whether or not a belief system is based upon reality is something that people need to check out, to investigate, to determine. What we tend to forget sometimes in accepting others is that while we can and should accept that they have different belief systems—we can do so without believing their beliefs. Our society has become more prone to condemn those who believe in only one system, calling it a form of hatred against those with other beliefs. The opposite is actually the case. It is only when I respectfully understand that others have their own beliefs, while I have mine, that I am truly accepting others as unique individuals and anticipate being treated as one myself. The Earth is smaller than the sun, $22 + 6 = 28$, and I believe my faith to be based on facts or I wouldn't believe it. I don't hate anyone who disagrees and I hope not to be hated for disagreeing.

Actually, I don't hate anyone at all. Those who have discarded their humanity to hate others and have acted despicably in the process are not to be admired. I choose, however, not to respond in hatred. The old adage "Two wrongs don't make a right" rings true. To hate is to harden my heart and make it too hard to love. There is no Joy in hatred. That isn't the lesson of being "backwards" or my own person. It is a related lesson, though, and one that leads us closer to truly letting go of those things that steal our Joy in life.

Once you start discovering all of the things that make you uniquely you and you aren't threatened by doing them differently, it's kind of fun to really explore the differences. What isn't fun is changing yourself to match others, denying what you really believe or feel. Or trying to make all of the people around you into clones so that they can't do or say or believe or feel.

When I taught my sons to tie their shoes, they got it "right" of course. Now, do I teach my future grandchildren so they get it "right" or do I continue the generational reversal so every other generation is "backwards?"

Joy comes in being happy with being you, but without needing to make others be you.

• L I F E   L E S S O N   3 •

"What If?"

I used to play "What If" with my gifted students. What if we all suddenly sprouted working wings? What if people never needed to sleep anymore? The students would work in teams to list as many separate ways in which life would change as they could think of in a few minutes time. Answers for the first one would include items like 1) We would need to redesign clothing in order for our wings to be free. 2) We would need to redesign furniture to make it comfortable with our new folded wings. 3) We would need an increase in clothing factories to catch up with making the clothes quickly. 4) The employment rate among clothing designers and manufacturers would rise. 5) There would be a decrease in vehicles as people began flying places. 6) There would be a decrease in employment for car manufacturers.

For the second question just picture one of my favorite answers—It sure would be tough for parents of newborns who never sleep. Yikes.

The game was intended to elicit the type of brainstorming that could lead to in depth understanding of situations. This leads to ideas for future innovations or to possible solutions to problems. All of this in the framework of a team. Interestingly enough, we played this game when I started teaching gifted back in the early 80's. It heartens me that I see major tech and design corporations working this way now. Education in this nation isn't as far back as many would like to paint it. As a matter of fact, there is a great deal of worth in the system, despite the need for change in some areas. That's a digression only in a way.

"What if" was a classroom exercise in thinking. Students discussed both the positive and negative ramifications of the setup I gave them. It was not a stressful situation, because it in no way related to their real lives. Some of them really wanted to sprout wings or not ever get tired, but it wasn't real.

Funny how people play this game with their real lives. Almost always with only the negative possibilities. "What if I catch the flu?" "What if I say the wrong thing?" "What if …" In our game, students couldn't list the same thing in different words, such as 1) new shirts 2) new coats 3) new blouses, etc. That's actually one answer—new clothing. However, they were encouraged to let one idea lead to another as in the new clothing leading to an increase of employment in the clothing industry. "What If" in real life tends to run this way as well. When I was in sixth grade I jammed my finger playing basketball. It hurt physically, but it was the game of What If that made it worse. What if I have to get a cast? What if I can't write and do my homework? What if I can't go to sixth grade camp? What if everyone at school makes fun of me for missing camp?

It was a silly set of assumptions. It was real to me, though. The more I thought, the more I stressed. Good news is that my two dear friends, Diane and Cathy, didn't let me stay on that silly thread of thoughts. As a matter of fact, they told me to stop it—that none of that stuff was going to happen and to chill out. It's good to have friends who tell it like it is when you need it. A little splint for a couple of days and I was as good as new.

I'm not speaking against planning or being prepared.

Planning in life is essential. How can I be ready with health care or be financially secure in case of sickness or loss of employment? Those are important questions for people. There are real situations that cause real concern.

The distinction here is between calmly preparing for real, possible situations or frantically worrying about possibilities that are unlikely or unchangeable. When the first "What If" is a possibility, however faint, but it leads to more and more improbable situations that bring stress, then you have stolen the Joy from your life.

Consider the "What if I say something dumb at this event?" scenario. This leads to worries about social isolation and fear of being alone. The game of "What If" when played out in life is essentially a game of fear—ungrounded, unreal fear.

There are solutions.

One solution is play the game through, but with realistic answers. Can I be careful of what I'm saying in a social situation that requires it? Can I listen carefully to others so that I can think through a reply? If even after listening and thinking, something doesn't come out quite right, does a hole open up in the floor and swallow me? If so, then there are a lot of very famous people from athletes to performers to politicians, who would have been falling through floors. Yet, they didn't. Everyone laughed and they moved on. Many times, they've explained what they've really meant, and people accept that humans sometimes do not clearly articulate what they really mean. It's life. For those of us not famous and not making the newscasts with our mixed up words, they will likely be forgotten pretty quickly. Life will move on. Will a silly statement really lead everyone to desert us? In my wonderful family and friends, we enjoy each faux pas that someone makes as a reason to laugh with them— just as they laugh with us when it's our turn. We know that we'll have a statement come out incorrectly sometimes. That's life. The mistake is a source of Joy instead of fear. Realistically, I know this isn't true in all families or friends.

Yet, I know people who have chosen friends who can laugh with them and enjoy their company.

Another solution is to switch to positive "What If's". What if I meet someone at this event that I can have a really great conversation with? What if I make a new friend, or perhaps a new business contact. What if I have an incredibly good time that I would have missed if I had stayed home. Focusing on the positive outcomes can overcome our fear of the negative ones. Students at our school give speeches to the whole middle school when they are in eighth grade. They choose a topic that they think is important and speak on it for eight to twelve minutes. Naturally, this can bring some nervousness. When I see the nerves, I tell the kids to focus on their message. They believe in what they are saying, and they can see it as an opportunity to help others understand the importance of it and help get things started to make the world a better place. It's not the perfect words that do that—it's their heart for it. There is no room for negative thinking in this positive approach.

Another consideration in moving to a different approach is that the fear of what might happen does not stop anything from happening. Most fears are ungrounded—they just steal your Joy in life. The fear that does happen, however, brings about a continued set of fears. The occurrence doesn't make the other anxieties more likely, it just makes them more fearful. When I was a kid, my parents taught me what to do in case of a tornado. My mom loves windows and designed a house totally surrounded in them—not the best case scenario for a tornado in Ohio. It scared me, even knowing what to do, even prepared, I was terrified whenever they predicted possible tornados in the area. I never saw one until I was in my late thirties. I was living in my own home with my husband and two sons and a sudden fierce storm hit while my husband was out at the store. I had lost my childhood fear by now and the thought of a tornado wasn't even on the radar. Then I heard that "train" sound they tell you about. This is where all the preparation in the world doesn't always lead you to the right reaction. I immediately ran to my front door to look out, instead of hurrying into a safe tornado position. Not the best idea under the circumstances, so I'm all the more grateful for how it turned out.

In the front yard of the home we had purchased was a huge evergreen. We had found out not long before that this tree was dying and should be removed, but we just couldn't do so at that time. As I got to the door, I saw a swirling, whirling wind pick that tree up out of the ground, spinning it before dropping it. I stood in amazement. The tree could have come right toward me and taken out our entire living room with me in it. If it had gone the opposite direction, the electric and telephone pole in front of our house along with the tree on our lawn would have likely ended up in the street. If it had fallen sideways, the neighbor's house or car could have been totaled. Instead, that tree came down right in between our van and our garage—without damaging either one. Soon after, my husband arrived home safely through the storm, as grateful as I was that we were all safe.

That little twister could have revived my old fear of tornados, but I know that it isn't likely that I'll see another in my lifetime. Look up the statistics on that one. Knowing that it's highly improbable helps me see that fear as just an old game of "What If" that can't be used for any good purpose for learning.

I think I'll stick to the positive. "What if my students can win the National Academic Championship?" I envision a ticker tape parade…

Is That Right?

If you ask most people if they live with integrity, they will answer yes, well-knowing the dictionary's definition of the word and fully applying it to their lives. It's funny how people can relate everything to themselves. The reason that this can work, of course, is because integrity is a very broad term. There are so many different types of actions that fall under this. We can take some of these actions as applicable and believe then that the whole term is therefore applicable.

In truth, I'm sure that we as humans fall short of the full definition of this word at times. It's not that we don't try or don't want to be people of integrity, it's just that…well, we live real lives. There's a sliding scale of integrity, from those who really don't care to do the right thing at all to those who live their lives trying at all times to do what is right and good. In that scale, there's always places where we all might not quite get it right. Part of living with integrity is in what we do then. It's another chance to choose to do what's right by choosing to admit our errors and work to repair the hurt we've caused.

Getting past the dictionary definition, then, I would describe integrity as doing the best thing when you can to make the world the best it can be for others, as well as yourself. The other day I went straight to the service counter of the store when I walked in. I asked the gentleman waiting in line next if I could quickly cut in just to let the woman behind the counter know that there was a car with its lights on in a handicapped spot out front. He let me in but told me that he believed that if they left their lights on, they deserved to be without power when they got back. I worried about a handicapped person returning to a dead car, while he felt that they probably weren't even handicapped, just putting that on there to get the space. We came from two different directions on the situation—because what we thought was right came from a perspective of whether or not someone needed help or not. By my definition, I'll always err on the side of helping because it may be needed. However, that doesn't mean I always get it right.

I give that intro before the story that leads up to the lesson in living with integrity, lest you think that I'm trying to claim sainthood. I believe whole-heartedly that the more integrity we live with, the more joyful we'll be. I'm not claiming perfection. When I fall short, I need others around me to help me get back up and do what I should do.

It was seventh grade and our math teacher, the incomparable Mr. Snow, had promised us all ice cream if everyone got a perfect math test sometime during the year. In the warmth of those final days of school, this funny and brilliant man gave us an easy one. We knew right away the intent and we rushed through the problems busily writing while thinking of ice cream. Instead of handing it in, he had us exchange tests and grade them as he gave the answers. Every hand went up when he asked how many had gotten them all correct. As he headed down to the cafeteria freezer to get our ice cream, I excitedly whispered to my dear friend, Diane, about getting the ice cream. She surprised me. "We aren't getting ice cream." I assured her we were, so she rephrased it. "I'm not getting ice cream, I don't know about you."

She went on to explain that someone in the hurry had missed a problem near her, but that the person who had graded it had marked it right so that we could get ice cream. She would not take the treat under false pretenses. Now I had a choice to make. Did I go with her on what was right and get everyone in the class mad at me? Or did I go against one my best friends and against what I knew was right? I didn't like either option honestly. Mr. Snow came in with a whole box of those little ice cream containers with the peel off lids and a big smile on his face while the class cheered wildly. I wasn't that excited and I still didn't know what to do. Diane stood up and looked directly at me and then turned to walk to the front of the room. I knew what I had to do, and miserably I got up and followed her. She didn't make a scene, she didn't announce it loudly in some self-righteous tirade. She quietly whispered to him that we couldn't take the ice cream because someone had missed a question but didn't want to be the cause of everyone missing ice cream so nothing was said. She didn't even say who. I was, and am still, amazed at her integrity. Not only did she do the right thing—she did it in the right way. I just stood there with her. It wasn't the first time that Diane had been my conscience, and it wouldn't be my last. She knows how to say what needs to be said, and how to say it in a way that no one gets hurt. That's rare—and puts her near the top of that sliding scale if you ask my opinion. She will humbly deny it if you ask her. When I need to hear the truth even if it hurts, it's her number I call.

Mr. Snow was surprised—and pleased with this show of honesty. He rewarded Diane and me with an extra cup of ice cream without any fanfare. He then handed out the ice cream to the rest of the class without trying to discover who cheated and embarrass them. Seeing it now from a teacher's perspective, I realize that he knew he had set up the situation to treat the class and could not have expected anyone to admit to cheating under the circumstances without causing a problem. At the time, I only knew that I felt good about having done the right thing in the right way for the right reasons—and that I was eating an extra ice cream because of it. I didn't understand why it had happened the way it did entirely but I knew that I felt really happy. I had been taught by my parents to stand up and do what is right, even when the crowd does not, but this was living it. I was downright joyful.

Another example is in order here, but it will take just a little family history to make sense. When I was young, Aunt Sarah moved with her family to our little suburb of Cleveland. She wasn't my aunt yet, but then she and my mom became friends and she adopted the title. That's the way it was with several of my mom's friends—they became family. What was different here is that Aunt Sarah was a member of a large family in Cleveland who had started a Gospel choir, the Weeden Family singers. She sang with her brothers and sisters, their spouses, and their children. She came from a large family and her father, the Rev. John Weeden was the pastor of a great church on the east side of Cleveland. It didn't seem odd at the time that my mom joined the choir and began singing with the family so that we joined the Weeden family. Now I see it as amazing and wonderful. I soon had lots of extra aunts, uncles, and cousins. I had an extra Christmas celebration each year and lots more people loving me. If you want to make a kid extra happy, add family members for all special occasions. The added icing on this cake? I now had another set of grandparents. Having two incredible sets already, this was just the best! Granddaddy and Grandma Weeden loved on us. I was young and it never occurred to me, even in the 60's and 70's, that people would think it odd that a little white suburban girl would have black grandparents. When I did encounter confusion or hostility later in life, it was easy to just laugh it off. Family always meant more to me than the feelings of strangers, so it didn't matter.

I'm not really talking about my personal integrity here though. There are others that showed great integrity to me, so that I could learn to live with honor and not care about what the world thought right. My parents, of course, showed me that all people are people and laughed when people reacted. Then there was Granddaddy. I didn't know it at the time, for he was a man clothed in humility, but he was one of the civil rights leaders in the area. On the wall behind my desk at school, I have a picture of him in 1964 marching in downtown Cleveland with other area leaders and Dr. Martin Luther King Jr. He looks so serious in the picture. Normally he was smiling and laughing with Joy—infectiously so. When they talk about having a twinkle in your eye, they're talking about Granddaddy. I never felt like I was an add-on grandchild. I was his granddaughter and he loved me. He loved people, he loved life. I see the picture and I realize that he was serious because he knew that marching for what was right was serious business. Marching could mean being beaten, being hosed with the overpowering spray from fire hoses, being hit with bricks or other heavy objects thrown at him. It could mean being killed. Thankfully, it was not that way in Cleveland and they marched safely. However, doing the right thing could have cost him everything. There were other marches in other cities he went to with Dr. King. He did it anyway. That's integrity.

As serious as he looks in the picture, Granddaddy Weeden had great Joy in living life the way it should be lived. I don't think that he would have had the same Joy if he hadn't been doing what he could to make the world a better place.

That's how I want to live too—at the highest end of the integrity scale. I want to know those depths of Joy and share it with others.

• LIFE LESSON 5 •

How Come You Get to Be
Perfect When I Can't Be?

I've learned a lot from my students over the years. Gifted students have such remarkable thought processes. My job is so much fun and I love working with these kids who can analyze and think to such depth. They ponder, they cogitate, they consider. They see the endless possibilities that many never consider.

Then they get upset.

In seeing those possibilities, they determine the best possible outcome—the perfect solution, resolution, state of being. They see themselves and the world as it should be.

But it isn't.

In their frustration, nearly half of them work endlessly trying to reach that perfection. They give themselves, and those around, headaches and stomachaches and panic attacks. The other near half quit trying because they've concluded that there is no point when you can't get it perfect anyway—so why bother? They have the ability, but the work isn't getting done. The final percent are those in the middle who are able to find the balance and find a more joyful way to live.

I've spent my career helping the first two groups find a happy medium.

I ask you here what I've asked many students over the

last forty years of teaching, as I try to help them find that balance that will bring them far more Joy in their lives.

"What is the difference between perfect and excellent?"

Most of the students, and doubtless many of you, answer this question with, "One is better than the other." It's okay if you failed this quiz. It wasn't graded and does not count towards your GPA.

The correct answer is, "One is achievable."

The other is not.

We do not live in a perfect world. We are not perfect. That causes a lot of problems, of course. Then again, I tend to analyze this backwards. It is our imperfections that make us not only human, but different. If we were all perfect, we could all do everything. How boring it would be if everyone could play the piano or write plays or paint the perfect painting or sing a song that would bring tears to your eyes or write the best of books on living joyfully. As a matter of fact, nothing anyone did would be of any value because everyone else could do exactly the same thing. Perhaps we'd all have the worst egos and be insufferable and uncaring because we would see ourselves as having the greatest value on earth. Conversely, we might feel completely unfulfilled because there would be no way to showcase our own abilities.

Picture yourself at work or school sitting next to someone who is perfect. They do everything exactly right. They do all of the work without a single error, they know exactly the right thing to say at the right time. Are they impressive? Heroic? Ready to be idolized? Tell me something. Would you even like that person? I've never had anyone tell me that they would. So why would we want to be that person?

Excellence is possible. We should all absolutely strive for it. You just have to remember that it is not equally possible for everyone in all subjects. Mozart, on the bell curve of musical ability, was somewhere way out on the far end of the bell. The man was highly gifted in this area of life. I'm not sure in which areas of life he had his weaknesses, but I know that on some bell curve, he was sitting on the opposite side of the bell. For on every bell curve for every ability in life, there are people on both ends even while most are in the middle. This is why we appreciate the people with the great ability – because they are unique in what they can do. I also know that everyone has great strengths on some curve and weaknesses on others.

I was asked to stand on the end of the row in choir in junior high and lip sync so I would stop throwing people off key. Seriously. In college I had to take a music class for teachers. My poor teacher soon learned that I understood it all in some intellectual way but that I could no more figure out what it meant it terms of putting it together than I could sprout those wings my students like to consider in "What if." She asked me not to be offended when she explained the obvious: I'm tone deaf and have no sense of rhythm. I asked her to grade me on effort and promised to never teach music. Mozart and I are holding down the opposite ends of that curve.

I'm okay with that. I have other gifts that work well for me. I applaud people for the gifts they have. It's such an incredibly diverse world and there is so much Joy in admiring the works that others can create.

These differences extend to even how we learn and accomplish tasks. I give learning styles tests to my students. I've taken them myself. Knowing how we think and learn is vital sometimes to accomplishing tasks. Some learn best by reading, but others by hearing or seeing or moving objects. Some need the whole concept at once before breaking down in pieces while others want the step by step so they can get the big idea. The latter group tends to understand the math the way it is taught more readily than the first, while the former would do well to study completed math problems before working out steps.

Why tell you all of that? Well sometimes our frustration is in trying to accomplish what others are accomplishing and in the way they are doing it. The fact is that we need to determine what our abilities are and how we can best use them. You can change neither your learning style nor your gifts. You can use your strengths to learn how to use your abilities to accomplish things you can do extremely well. Then we can go for the life where we are using the gifts we have and enjoying our accomplishments. It doesn't mean that we can't learn things other than our strengths with hard work. It can't be used as an excuse to not try something. It does mean that we have the most Joy when we are pursuing what we find comes most naturally to us.

We can also appreciate people with the gifts they have and see them as such. There is no Joy in envying others. No gift is better than another, no human worthy of more or less respect based on whether their gifts place them in or out of the spotlight. There have been a couple of wonderful women who have been cutting my thick, too-curly, frizzy hair for many years. They are highly gifted in knowing exactly what to do. It amazes me. They can look at this mop and see what it should be and then make it that way. (No, I'm not telling you where to find these gifted stylists—they already have full schedules). The service people who keep all of those parts working on my car so that I never have to worry about breaking down in the middle of nowhere— how on earth does anyone do anything mechanical? I don't get it. Athletes even at the school level amaze me. I couldn't get a good grade in P.E. when I was in school. I love swimming but I'm not ever going to compete with someone who has skill. I recently had a broken foot and had to have someone push me in a wheelchair through the Cleveland and Chicago airports when I took my students to an Academic Challenge competition. I felt awful about having to have someone take care of me like that. However, I was blessed by having two airport employees who put me at ease and went the extra mile to make me feel better and to ensure that my students and I stayed together and got to where we needed to be—all with a smile and an attitude that made a difficult situation so much easier. I am indeed grateful that these two "people" people are serving those of us who need them so much. The eye doctor who gave me steroid shots in the eyes for years has great depth of knowledge and was able to give me a breadth of information about my particular form of arthritis that was causing the problem and discuss it all with me. Then, he was able to give me the treatments I had to have with great skill.

All of these people are imperfect human beings in an imperfect world. They are all achieving excellence.

So can we.

When you look at the world and you see what should be, do you get discouraged because it isn't there? That's a common reaction. But it isn't the only one. Another reaction would be to, as you, do what you can to improve it. To strive for that excellence without giving up. Maybe, just maybe, if we all work together and do our little part with Joy, then most of it can be solved. Not all of course—we're still imperfect.

Years ago, I had a few students at my desk waiting to discuss a graded test they had gotten back. It was very early in my career—later I would only discuss grades when no other student was up there to hear the conversation – but I hadn't quite gotten that yet. The first student was stressing over a B+. I told her that the sun would rise in the morning. Her loving parents would still be there, she would have clothes to wear, food to eat, friends who cared, and a great future. And absolutely no one in her future would know about the grade or care. It would have no relevance whatsoever to her future (I'm not a big fan of grades, there are better ways to help students focus on what they need to learn without making the grade more important than life). As she continued to argue, the student behind her piped in. "Would you sit down and be quiet? I'm here to discuss a D." The remark put it into perspective. Both needed to focus on what they could do, work to achieve it, aim for excellence, and not stress about not being perfect.

So do we all.

I also tell you this, as I tell my students when they begin the perfectionism stuff.

You can be perfect when I get there. Don't hold your breath.

• LIFE LESSON 6 •
When Life is Tough

L ife is funny sometimes. People say it all the time, usually when something isn't funny at all. It's said when something difficult and unexpected happens. Just one of those clichés that people throw in when they have no idea what to say in the situation.

That's okay.

At least they're saying something in response to the situation. They're attempting to connect with someone who is hurting. And the person who is hurting will feel better if they accept the effort with the concern and care it conveys, instead of rankling at the cliché.

There are times when people think that my joyful life is indicative of a life that has not encountered difficulty. There is no such life on this earth. We don't live in a perfect world. I have had a wonderful life but it has not been pain-free—physically or emotionally. My husband and children are incredible and fill my life with such love and Joy. I have fantastic family and friends, a job I love, a good home. Yet I lived through crippling arthritis for many years, extreme nearsightedness, and eventually eye shots when the arthritis affected my eyes. I lost a child when I was four months pregnant. My first marriage fell apart right around the ten year mark when our son was four. I lost my beloved sister when she was only fifty-one. I lost my Dad last year, and although I am grateful for all the years I had him, it does not make me miss him less. I'm giving the highlights of the lowlights here.

So how to live a joyful life when the pain is beyond understanding?

When my youngest son was eight years old he was diagnosed with diabetes. He ended up in pediatric intensive care and I slept on a cot next to him for several days as he recovered. My husband would go to work, come to the hospital with us, and then go home for a little sleep before starting again the next day. Needless to say, we were all exhausted fairly soon. We barely had time to process let alone time to talk, time to pray, time to consider this drastic change in our lives. Somewhere around day 3 or 4, I took my bleary-eyed self out of the room to go down to the cafeteria to get something to eat. I paused at the desk to ask a question and was stopped by another mother. She asked why my child was in the hospital and I grimly told her. Her response brought me back to reality. "Thank God that that's all he has. My daughter is dying of leukemia." She was so right. When I got back to the room, Alex and I thanked God that he was going to be alright. I also prayed for her and her daughter.

No matter what has happened in my life, there are people who have had it so much harder. I had eye problems? There are many who cannot see. I'm neither blind nor arthritic. I lost a baby? I know people who have lost more than one and some who have not been able to have children when they wanted them desperately and people who have lost children after they were born which I know is far worse. I have been married for twenty-eight incredible years to my husband and we gave my oldest a little brother. My sister had twenty-three incredible, wonderful extra years with me after a remarkable kidney transplant lasted far longer than normal. And through all of this, there were people there to comfort me, to mourn with me, to love me.

It's not that hard things never happen, but that mother in the hospital was right. In the midst of the pain, what can I be thankful for?

I'm not one that generally lives by lists of how to live, but there are times when they can be useful to help us separate out the ideas. So I offer this list of getting through the pain back to Joy.

1) Know that life here can never be perfect. If you don't expect perfect, you aren't shocked when the imperfect causes you pain. The world is not perfect but it has so many good things to offer that when the hard comes along we can be shocked.

2) Remember that no problem or pain that happens to you is new to mankind; sorrow has stretched through every generation of people from the beginning.

3) Remember that no matter how hard it is, there are people who have gone through the pain or worse. You are not alone. Things could be worse, even while you know they could be better.

4) Be thankful that they aren't worse.

5) Surround yourself with people who care and let their love uplift you. Find someone who can listen when you want to speak and cry with you when you need to cry. Do not be upset if they use clichés to help you. Remember they are trying without knowing exactly what to say.

6) Listen to good advice. Sometimes things are fixable if we know how to solve them – and others may know of resources to help us—medically, financially, emotionally, etc.

7) Do not listen to those who are negative. Do not believe that things can't get better and don't listen to those who do believe that. Do not let others make it worse.

8) Remember that sorrow is not forever. Grief, pain, fear and worry are real but they are not all life has to offer. Remember the good things. Hang on until you can see them again.

9) For those of you who believe in God, let Him hold you and comfort you. His Love heals great sorrow. Pray and ask others to pray for you as well.

At the time of the pain, it's hard to remember that the pain will fade over time, and you will laugh again. You will when you can look at the good in life and realize that although life isn't perfect, it is good. There are so many awesome, wonderful, beautiful things in life that are forgotten when the sorrow hits. Look for them. Look for them with others.

I know that #5 hits hard for some. They are alone. They have lost family and friends. If you are alone, look for a place with people who can help you. My sister worked for a hospice for seventeen years. When she passed away, hundreds of people came to comfort us, many of whom we had not met but who wanted to say how much she had helped them through their own losses. There are organizations, people, and places who will help in what you are going through—seek them out. You do not have to bear the grief without hope or help. There are people who understand your pain because they have lived it and come through it. Many of these organizations and groups cost nothing but you can gain everything. I know many recommend finding a place to volunteer where you can help others and be with others. Volunteering enriches us all and it's a good idea. Sometimes, however, we need to get some help with some healing of our own before we are ready to help others. These are not either/or. You can find someone to help you while you help others. Only you know what you need most here, but the help doesn't always come to you. Find those places where your healing can happen. Finally, if there are people who have been trying to help you but you haven't been ready to let them, consider not shutting them out. "I can do this myself" does not make one stronger, it robs us of the critical support system that we need when life hits hard.

There's more to #6 as well. When we are hurting, we can fall into a hopeless negative loop where we feel it can't be solved and we tune these people out without realizing that they may know an answer to pull us out of the trouble we're in. The pain and fear can make us not seek out solutions or not move on when we should. After my divorce, I moved back to Ohio and in with my sister for a while. For days, she held me while I cried, she listened, she comforted. She stayed up late and played video games with me (ahh, Frogger). She took me out late at night to lay in the back yard and look at the stars and talk. Somehow she got up for work early every morning and came home to take care of me. After a few days had passed, she woke me one morning with a map (no GPS or internet directions I could use in 1989). On it were circled the local boards of education. They were numbered to create the best route to hit them all in the shortest period of time.

She explained that I needed to get out there and get a job while it was still summer so that I could take care of myself and my son. I was feeling miserable but I got ready and went out while she headed for work. I came home late that afternoon with a contract for the next school year (I know it's not the norm, but it's the way it worked, thankfully). Her response was a hearty congratulations and the news that she had contacted her brother-in-law, the real estate agent, to find me a house. I was floored and protested that I couldn't possibly get a house. It was like arguing with the wind. Her brother-in-law knew exactly how to go about finding something that I could afford and that would be just the place for my son, Danny, and I. Within a couple of months, I was signing the mortgage on a nice home near my parents that came with a very doable first time home-owners special deal that I wouldn't have known about without the help. A few days later, my old car was replaced with something more reliable as my parents sent me off to find something that wouldn't break down with their grandson (and daughter) in it. There was a choice to be made in the midst of my pain, to let them help me to move on and to work my way out, or to wallow in the pain and not move out of it all. The latter would have kept me bound down but it also would have had lasting implications as to work, finances, living arrangements, transportation. In the end, it would also have caused far more serious issues for my son as well. I needed to get my life moving again for both us. It's not that it didn't hurt anymore for either of us but it gave us focus and means to start again. It may not be family members who help you when you are in your darkest hour but there are many out there who can and will help if you let them.

Let me also mention that if you know someone going through a difficult time in life that you can be the one who uplifts and cares. Each word or deed can be a lifeline to help bring someone a small step back from sorrow to Joy. Do you know of resources that may help? Can you offer a listening ear? Can you offer to help with something? When you reach out, it is like a lifeline to the drowning. Even if you don't know exactly what to say. Even if you use a cliché.

There is Joy in accepting comfort and in bringing comfort to others.

• LIFE LESSON 7 •

Oh, That's Who You Are!

Even in junior high, I knew better than to try out for the musicals. I loved drama, acting was just a blast. But when the choir teacher asks you to stand at the end of the line in choir and lip sync so that you quit throwing people off key, musicals are likely a bad choice. So I would be in the fall drama or comedy (or dramedy as most early teen dramas add a lot of unintended humor). I never did another tryout for the spring musical after a disastrous attempt in seventh grade.

I still worked the set building, the program creating, and of course the makeup crew. I had first watched my mom run makeup in a little theater in the area when I was really little. I loved it! You could totally create a person into a character. In junior high, it was even better because my friend, Carol, loved it too. We would start attending the rehearsals near production time and start planning out who would do what makeup for which character.

The fact that I hadn't gone to tryouts for the musical in the spring of 1971 meant that I didn't know that a girl who had just moved into our neighborhood and started coming to our school had tried out for and made the lead. She wasn't in any of my classes and I didn't even know she existed until one of the early dress rehearsals. As we watched, I was transfixed. Like a little girl watching a princess they admire, I saw her singing this song. When girls are small, we so often look at that beautiful princess and we are transported to that magical place of a world where we can be the beautiful princess and have a handsome prince come sweep us away to live in the castle of our dreams. Even tomboys like me could sometimes fall into this. This girl reminded me of that as she sang with this incredible voice and the music flowed from the stage.

Carol knew everyone, so I asked who the girl was. When the song ended, I went to the stage to compliment her—I almost felt like asking for an autograph as if I were in the presence of celebrity.

What happened next forever transformed my feelings about how I looked at people.

I reached out a hand to shake hers and I complimented her by telling her what a wonderful job she had done.

She tossed her hair back over her shoulder with a quick shrug and a toss and said, "Yes, I was wonderful, wasn't I."

In that one second, split second, millisecond…I realized that she wasn't really very pretty at all. I thought her features to be not quite right and her hair style not to be flattering. I saw her as quite un-beautiful.

She looked like a totally different person because she was totally different than what I had thought she was. My impression of her had been based upon how she looked and sang and I had created a character of who I thought she was based on those externals. It's just not who she really was.

Who she really was affected how I saw her. Though her pictures would have detected no difference, my judging heart saw one in real life.

And I was judging. I wasn't right to do so, it was how I determined which people I wanted to hang out with and be friends with. I sure didn't want to hang out with this girl. As time went on, lots of other kids felt the same way. It wasn't a school that fed snooty attitudes particularly well. She had a small clique of friends, but most weren't taking the time to befriend her.

Isn't that what we do in life? We judge others based on one act, one word, one look, how they look, how they react to us. We don't want to be judged that way, of course. We don't have any qualms about looking at others through that filtering lens, we just want others to see all of our best qualities and like us for them.

Do I know why she had the attitude that day? I don't. Maybe she really had a large ego or maybe she was hiding an insecurity about starting in a new school. I have no idea. Truth be told, I really knew very little about her. Although we went all the way through the rest of school together, I don't know who she really was. Did she like the same music? Did she like to play card games? Was she dreaming of being an actress when she grew older? Did she worry about the Cold War or the draft like most of us in those early 70's?

Maybe, if I had seen past that attitude, I could have had another friend to laugh through Drama Club together.

There are two lessons here—one for each of us.

The first lesson is from the singer who seemed to care most about herself. It is that when we develop attitudes or protective shells that we keep people away. There are lots of reasons for those shells. I've had many students with thick, tough shells and lots of anger. Generally, they've been hurt by those who should have loved and cherished them. Parents or caregivers who have been more concerned with self than child. Friends of the family who aren't beyond betraying those friendships. Babysitters, siblings, neighbors who have been mean or hurtful. Problems beyond their control or understanding even by family who loves them but who can't shield them from financial difficulties or family problems. Perhaps they have some sort of issue that has made them a target of others. Perhaps they talk differently or they walk differently or think differently or look differently. My thick glasses starting in first grade surely separated how my classmates thought of me and how they treated me. One classmate reminded me daily how I "looked funny in glasses" sending me home in tears. I withdrew into quietness, becoming a book worm who found it easiest just to avoid contact at school. Thankfully, Diane and Cathy were my neighbor friends—at home and at school—but the rejection at school by a few affected my whole experience and how I got along with others. I'm not naturally quiet and retiring but that's how I acted until I got contacts at the beginning of junior high and finally starting talking to everyone. The sad thing is that I almost felt like the contacts made me a different person so that I could act differently. My glasses were my shell.

Doubtless, there were those who must have thought me arrogant or aloof.

I was just hurt.

Did she have a shell also? One we couldn't see at the school? Was she taught that she was better than the rest of us and believe it? If that's the case, she was still hurt—but in a different way. She had learned to separate herself from other humans and could never share in those friendships. Either way, I hope that she was able to make those friends as an adult that she missed as a student.

The second lesson is from my judgmental reaction. Those who judged me kept me from showing my better self and kept us all from forming possible friendships. Let me be honest then and admit that I have affected others negatively by judging them. I am not proud of that.

I would have smugly told you if confronted that I was not judgmental at all. Growing up in a liberal and mixed family, I hadn't learned to judge people by appearance or race or religion or any of the usual parameters. Yet, just one more glance at the story above tells a different story. I judged others for being uncaring, egotistical, and judgmental. Yes, that made me judgmental. It made me just as "bad". I just didn't see that at the time. I cannot say that I do not get upset when I hear people judging others even now. I will never agree with it. But I cannot determine that the people saying it are inhuman and not worthy of real conversation that may lead to the cracking of the "shells" that are causing the judgment. Maybe we can all learn to stop judging.

Which of these is the chicken and which the egg? This is a cycle. The attitudes and hurts bring negative behaviors that many around have no understanding of nor understanding of how to cope with. The resulting reaction pushes people further into their retreat or attack, in whatever form it takes. This causes more negative behaviors which cause…

Whichever is first, we can stop the cycle by interrupting it.

We can choose first impressions in both directions. First, we can choose how we act when we meet people. It's when we try to put on an act for new people that we are most likely to act in a way that puts them off. Most don't need some sort of false pretense. Are we acting in self-protection, fear, worry? It's not that we lay our lives out on the line to those we meet, but that we react with genuine interest in meeting someone and just relax. Saying that is easier than doing it of course. The reason? Most people are afraid someone won't like them, so they aren't sure what to do. They might pull back or overreact and people may not like the response. We have another chicken and egg. Instead of pulling back or overreacting, we can step back to decide that whether or not someone likes us on first meeting is not the end of the world. Nor does their impression of us affect who we are. Knowing this allows us to relax a bit. Do you have family, friends, or people who care about you as you are? Then the rest of the world doesn't have to think you're the best. Your worth is not based upon the opinion of strangers or being universally loved. Some will like us and some will not. Let them like us for who we are and not who we pretend to be. It may take some work but you can internalize the idea that your value is not based upon meeting more people. Once you get there, you can be yourself when you meet others and not stress about the impression you'll give.

Oddly enough, it is sometimes easier to stop the negative thoughts based upon your first impression of others than it is to stop worrying about what others think about us. Remembering that they may be reacting based upon the same feelings of fear and worry that others face helps. Realizing that first impressions of us or others are often wrong helps. Deciding to give others a second chance works. It's a decision, not just an emotional response.

Sometimes the second chance leads to a new friendship. Sometimes, however, we find that the second and the third impression are still sour for us. That's okay. Everyone in life doesn't need our approval to have their value either. Maybe the person really does have too large of an ego for us or they really are angry or hate-filled people. We can look for the reasons behind someone's selfish, mean, or spiteful behavior and feel bad that they are choosing that route while recognizing that we they may not want to change and let go of the things that have caused the anger and hatred. The fact is that we are evaluating our ability to get along with that person based upon real information about them instead of a fleeting glimpse. Note that this is still not judging, still not saying that someone doesn't deserve to live or have friends or meet new people. We can decide that we do not want to spend time with someone without making a value determination about them as humans.

Looking at people as individuals and not judging them also relates to other factors far beyond attitude and first impressions. I have two pictures that I sometimes show groups of students. One is of a man in an FBI jacket standing at a bank counter. The other is of a man with some disfigurement on one side of his face, neck, arm, and hand on that side. I ask them which of the men is a hero. They will inevitably point out the man in the FBI jacket. They realize the truth when they find out that their choice is a bank robber caught in the act, while the other man has all of the scars because he ran into a house fire and rescued a family. All the fairy tales of the handsome prince and the beautiful princess triumphing over the ugly giant (troll, witch, whatever) reflect what people believe in real life— that the value of a person is based upon their appearance and that whether they are good or evil is reflected in that. It's taken much further even with beliefs that people are "good" or "bad" based upon skin color, occupation, political or religious beliefs, etc. It is toxic when the person's ability and intelligence is thought of as inherent based upon their height, nationality, hair color, age, or gender. Going a step further into discussion is basing the value of a human upon those abilities or upon their "success" in using those abilities to get "ahead" in life. This type of judgment automatically brings down those who do not fit the ideas of those who are "best" among us. We must value all human life in all our diversity, in who we are instead of who we aren't. There are obviously so many levels of judgment not even listed here. We must recognize it for what it is and let it go in order to let go of the anger and hurt that it causes.

Finally, these stereotypes are so deeply believed that not only do we judge based upon these factors but people can sometimes work hard to live up to this nonsense. There were girls in school who acted "dumb" to attract guys who thought girls, particularly blondes, weren't very bright. The relationships were not based on really knowing the real person, but on an acting job often by those who didn't think they were acting.

All of these snap judgements keep us away from other people based upon artificiality. It also keeps us from working well in this life with people who differ from what we want them to be. More than that, it affects how we feel about ourselves and how we should act.

Do you want others to stop judging you? Do you want to stop judging others? Be yourself, and let them be themselves.

There is no Joy in judgement.

• LIFE LESSON 8 •
You're Kidding? Right?

I had my back to the second grade class while writing on the board in those days before white boards. Soon I heard my one sweet, talkative, young second grader whispering to his neighbor. I didn't even turn around—just called his name and asked him nicely to quiet down and listen for a moment until I had finished my explanation. His surprised voice called out, "How'd you know it was me?" I turned and explained that teachers are born with eyes in the back of their heads—that's how we know we're going to be teachers. They all looked startled, but no one questioned me. Although they were the youngest group of gifted students I had worked with in the whole three years I had been teaching, I assumed they would know I was kidding.

A while later, I was sitting and reading to the class while they busy drawing or writing or just listening. My students are free to lay on the floors or desks, or sit, or whatever and multitask if they want—as long as they are listening. Most listen better that way actually. Remember that lesson that talked about learning styles? It's good to know if you learn best in silence or with music or with the TV on in the background (as I'm doing right now – I can't work in quiet or music). The students need to learn it, too. As I was

39

reading, one young lady got up to get something and I suddenly felt her fingers going through the back of my hair. I stopped, of course, to inquire why. Her reply with pouted lip, "You lied to us. You don't have eyes back here."

I never thought they would take me seriously. Honest.

But that's the way words are. Words have power; they affect people. They have meaning – and sometimes they mean something different to the person hearing them than the person speaking them. What you say in jest may not be taken that way. You don't mean offense, but someone is hearing something entirely different than what you meant.

And sometimes, I'll admit it even if no one else does, the words I've said have meant to offend. Sometimes they were taken that way, and sometimes they weren't. Either way, the intent was to use words as a weapon.

So maybe we should just all be silent.

Not that it would solve the problem. Non-verbal communication can cause the same problems. So there must be better solutions.

Just as in the lesson on first impressions, the solution is two-fold, depending on which side of the words you happen to be on.

The side of the speaker is an obvious solution. Think just a moment before you speak. Who are you speaking to? Do they know you well? Do they know you're someone who kids around? Are you kidding around?

There are so many different senses of humor. What one person finds hysterically funny leaves others shaking their heads. Unless you are a stand-up comic who is getting paid to be funny with people you don't know at all, that can be precarious ground to stand on. Someone may not know you're even joking or they may not find it to be humorous.

I had lunch duty with middle school students. It wasn't my lunch time and I was needed to walk around the cafeteria and keep order. So I walked, but watching people eat is not the most exciting activity, so I would stop at random tables of students I knew and make a joke here and there. One day

I stopped by a table and stated in a fake British accent, "Hello, I'm Mrs. Smythe, and I'll be your waitress for this luncheon. Would you care for a glass of hemlock with your meal." Several students immediately ordered the hemlock laughingly, while one student whispered to another, "What's hemlock?" His friend replied, "It's a poison. Just order it." The student looked even more bewildered than before. I kept on wandering between tables. A few minutes later, one of the students called out to me. "Oh, Miss. Please this way." I approached the table, and he pointed out the obvious. "We never got our glasses of hemlock at this table." I told him, "Oh, I'm terribly sorry, sir. We've discontinued the hemlock. The tips were lousy, and we didn't get any return customers." We all laughed, but I realized too late that the one student seemed still confused. I hadn't explained the joke, and now he was feeling like an outsider. It was okay to joke with the students. It wasn't okay to leave him on the outside feeling bad about not getting the joke. I could have, and should have, explained to him that I was kidding. I had another student at another table ask me if I was ever normal. I told him on the fifteenth Tuesday of each month. He replied that he didn't think that ever happened. I told him that's when I was normal.

When we are trying to be funny, we can make people feel less than smart—even when that isn't true. Many of my gifted students over the years might find something funny that others didn't. It's okay as long as you're noticing the cues of the listener and not pushing them to be amused too.

Of course, sometimes we're not trying to be funny. We're trying to be cutting or hurtful. I used to pride myself on my ability to put people "in their place" if I thought they were wrong. I didn't care who they were. If I thought they were wrong, I worked to bring them down a peg or two. When I was a sophomore in high school, I had the privilege of having my father as my biology teacher. It was his seventeenth year of teaching at the local high school. In those years, an incredible number of students had not only learned science, but had learned to care about their lives, their futures, and to care about others. He had literally changed lives. That sophomore year also brought new administrators to the school. Administrators make all the difference in the atmosphere of a school and by the end of that year a lot of teachers decided to go elsewhere, including my dad.

I was angry, resentful, accusatory. I was, however, a "good" hard-working student. I was in National Honor Society, student council, drama, etc. I was a student leader, so I didn't just do some rebellion. I planned out my response. Carol and I started an underground newspaper. In it, I mocked the principal and assistant principal. I accused them of cowardice and stupidity in what I thought was witticisms and intelligent satire. I know it hurt them, as they strove to find out the source of the paper. I carefully kept that hidden from them, even as I started to more openly oppose them. The day after the Supreme Court struck down dress codes, I wore shorts to school and boldly walked into the office in violation of our dress code. When confronted, I offered to go to court to discuss it. I could probably write pages and pages but it all leads to the fact that I treated these two people with contempt. There is no doubt that they rejoiced the day I graduated. They were let go the following year and I never saw either again.

Funny thing—none of that behavior brought my father back to the school he loved. In the long run, I was left knowing that I had used the words in that newspaper as weapons wielded against two people that I disagreed with. I had dehumanized them in my mind and justified it all. But I was not a better person for it. In fact, I was no better than others who use words to dehumanize people that I would disagree with. I had dehumanized *me* most of all. At first, I thought I was having fun but I wasn't left being joyful—far from it.

I was a young teenager when the former Governor George Wallace was shot. I saw it on the news and I cheered. I thought of him as a symbol of all the racism of the civil rights era and despised him for it. My father immediately stopped me from cheering. He told me that we do not rejoice in the harming of another human being, even if they are hateful people. If we do, we are being hateful—we are being just like them. I immediately sobered and stopped rejoicing. I didn't want to be hateful.

My parents obviously weren't in on how I was treating the high school administration for those two years. I obviously hadn't learned my lesson yet. There are always ways to justify when we are tearing others down. We give reasons that are perfectly plausible. The fact is that I still don't agree with the way these administrators ran the school. I don't. That doesn't change the fact that I was wrong. When we react that way, we are being bullies towards others. Bullies don't generally think they're bullies—they think that they are defending themselves (and sometimes others) when they are actually trying to exert power over others to harm them physically, mentally, and emotionally. They think of it as justice, power, and strength.

It doesn't bring peace or Joy.

To my high school administrators, if you are reading this, I don't know where you are but I am sorry for my behavior towards you. Please forgive me.

Good words have power also.

I haven't forgotten the listener viewpoint. You can decide that the person who has just made the remark or joke is an offensive idiot and get offended. Or you can ask what was meant and see if you were hearing what was said. If the person meant something other than what you heard then it all works out. If not...

Sometimes, you find out that they are definitely being offensive, and sometimes you know it for sure without even asking. If they did say something offensive, then you have a different choice to make.

At one point in high school, I stopped to get gas while out with two friends, one white and one black. Just three teenage girls who had been to the mall shopping and who were heading home laughing. For those of you born after the 1970's, there were actually people at gas stations who pumped the gas for you, took your cash, and gave you change. Hard to imagine, I know, but true. But it didn't go according to plan that evening. The guy who pumped my gas threw my change in my face and spat out the n-word! We were all shocked for a moment, and then Mickey, my black friend, started to laugh. She said, "Pat, why didn't you ever tell me you were black?" That's when the other friend and I cracked up.

Now, I guess we could have yelled at the kid. We knew he was wrong, we hadn't mistaken his words. Yet, don't we know that responding with offense would not have changed his mind? We could either let his ignorance bring us down or we could do what Mickey did. We could decide that his words had no power over us. We showed that he did not affect us. She chose an empowering response to the situation.

There are other empowering responses. My dad chose to go to the gas station manager when I told him about it that evening. He let the manager know how disappointed and upset he was by the situation. The manager chose to back up his worker and my father let him know that we would no longer be purchasing gas at his station and would encourage others to avoid it as well. He didn't cuss him out, or rant and rave. Those words would have been used to justify their actions. "See what *those people and their friends are like.*"

Dr. King, my Granddaddy, and other civil rights leaders showed the depth of their characters by knowing that violence begets violence and that hatred returned for hatred just makes the hatred grow. They responded peacefully and lovingly, changing hearts and lives and the world in the process. They did not let the offensive words of others embitter them.

It's alright to avoid situations or people who tend to be

toxic or offensive. It's alright to let people know that you do not agree with offensive things that are said. What isn't right is allowing it to drag you down into such anger that you are affected by someone else's animosity. We must always consider whether we want to become just like those toxic people or become the antidote.

When you feel the response coming on, filter for a moment. Is there a way in the situation you are in, to speak words of positivity? Is there a way to empower all to come out of the situation better, or at the least for you not to come out worse?

The pause can also give you an opportunity to be careful to not unintentionally offend someone.

There is no peace in bitterness and offense. There is no real Joy to be found there.

• LIFE LESSON 9 •
Have Fun, But Play Nice

To my beautiful niece, Mandi. I need to tell you how I really feel. Cabbage Patch dolls can be described as…not so good-looking, um…not really pretty. Well… I would say they're kind of ugly. I know you loved all your little "babies" when you were little, no matter how they looked. Bless you for not judging by outside appearance. I am really glad that my real great-nephews are exceptionally cute and take after you and Dave instead of after their older "siblings".

Please don't be offended if you love Cabbage Patch dolls. I don't mean any disrespect. They are terrific toys— well-loved by generations of kids. Their funny little faces are what makes them unique and different and their own cool brand. Their lack of beauty makes them sort of cute in an odd way. A very odd way.

Which is why my sister's practical joke was so funny.

My oldest son was born in Washington, D.C. My excited family drove out from the Cleveland area (yes, Cleveland, Ohio) to visit. Dad came out with my sister and brother-in-law and their two small children—my incredible niece and nephew. Poor Mom had to work and flew out a couple of days later extremely anxious to hold her 11-day-old grandson. Back then, you could actually walk out to the gate and drop people off or pick them up. So we eagerly waited for my mom to step off the plane while I held Danny.

I have no idea where she came from, but suddenly my sister, Betty, was in front of me and with lightning speed had taken Danny and left a wrapped baby blanket in my arms. Then she was gone. I was blurting out a question when I saw Mom rushing my way. Before I could move, she had the baby blanket and had opened it up with great excitement. I've never heard that kind of gasping scream before. I looked down to see Mandi's Cabbage Patch doll in our arms.

As my mother was demanding to know why I had scared her like that, we heard my sister giggling behind a column. I was trying to stutter that I hadn't been involved and that it wasn't my fault, but Mom could only see that I was holding the doll after all. How could I not have been involved?

I really wasn't involved but I sure wish we had had a camera for the look on her face when she opened that blanket. I kind of wish I had thought of it. Yet I know that I likely wouldn't have been able to pull it off very well.

In my family, I'm sort of the inadvertent practical joke helper. It's so much fun even if I don't know what I'm doing sometimes. Being part of the joke intentionally or unintentionally, or being the perpetrator (or co-conspirator) or (more commonly) the victim—it was all fun.

When my oldest was in elementary school, he asked for a Talk Boy (an early recorder for those younger than Baby Boom) for Christmas after watching Home Alone. It was THE gift of the season. We got it for him, but in the shopping process I had this crazy idea. We got him a ventriloquist dummy that looked just like Charlie McCarthy, the dummy made famous with Edgar Bergen in the 30's and 40's.

Now, you don't want a kid to know exactly what they're getting for Christmas, so we buried the Talk Boy in a very large box. We just didn't wrap it alone…nor did we leave it blank. We put twenty minutes of silence on it and then…

We woke Danny and our youngest, Alex, up and got them out to the living room to unwrap gifts. Before they could get there, I reached into a carefully opened corner at the bottom back of the box and turned it on. We started taking turns opening presents, oohing and aahhing and enjoying each item, while Danny eyed his big box awaiting the chance to find out what was in it.

All of the sudden, the box began to yell, "Let me out of here! Let me out of here!" Danny looked really startled and gave a worried glance at the huge box that was nearly twice as tall as he was. A moment later, the box again begged for release. We told him that he'd better open it. He found Charlie first and looked really confused. He was smart enough to know that it couldn't talk without human intervention. We had to encourage him to look again to find that we had wrapped two presents in one box.

It was a blast!

No mothers or children were harmed in the process of playing these practical jokes.

That's the point.

Jokes and pranks are supposed to be funny. I worry when I see someone who finds it funny to humiliate, embarrass, anger, or harm someone else. I worry when I see how society has made it hysterical to watch someone get hurt or humiliated. It devalues people. Real Joy is found in sharing it with others, not in their hurt.

Many years ago, I was invited to a rather formal dinner party where there were many important people. I wanted to make a good impression and arrived ready to enjoy an excellent evening. The host had told his wife that he would take care of all the details of the dinner and he did all of the cooking. As we all sat down to eat, he described each dish in detail and how it was cooked. It was like a very nice cooking show. The dishes were made with fine ingredients and the plates were beautiful.

The problem was that every dish had been carefully

prepared so that I could not eat any of it. I have an allergy to citric acid (vitamin C) in larger quantities. He had put orange peels and orange juice in the preparation of the dishes and/or sauces as well as serving a type of meat that I didn't eat at the time. The piece de resistance was the wine he served with no water on the table—I don't drink.

When I realized that I could eat or drink absolutely nothing on the table, I looked up at the host in shock. Now, mind you, I don't mind a practical joke. If at that point he had laughed and said, just kidding, of course you can eat it, I would have laughed, too. But he didn't. He just laughed. It actually took him a minute to realize that I was humiliated, embarrassed, angry, and upset. I was also hungry. I didn't want to make a scene in front of everyone, so I didn't say anything. That's when his wife caught on to what was happening and invited me back to the kitchen with her, where we made ourselves something else to eat and had a really nice time together.

It wasn't funny because it hurt someone—me.

Many people who find it funny to see other people get hurt would be offended if someone wounded them, and would be upset about others laughing at them if they were the injured party. It's really not funny. As my youngest says, I have an inherited empathy gene. My parents passed it on and even though it can be tough at times when I see others upset, I am very grateful for it.

That being said, they also gave me a well-developed sarcastic tone. My family loves dropping sarcastic and witty remarks all across the room at family gatherings. My younger brother seems to assert that I talk too much (wonder where he gets that idea?), while I recall how picky he's always been. We love each other to pieces, and we respect and admire each other. We're not trying to cause pain. And if my Dad thought that the teasing was going too far, he would step in. One day the whole group, including my two sons, kept picking on me for being "too nice". I was maintaining that the term is an oxymoron. Dad thought there were too many against one and jumped in to tell them to leave me alone. It was the way that he defended me that cracked us all up. He called me "a smart Edith Bunker"— for all you have never heard of *All in the Family*, you'll have to Google it. I wasn't sure if it was an insult or a compliment. It's all said in good fun and face-to-face, not behind each other's backs.

Learning when to use biting humor – not so easy. I look back and realized that too often I used it to belittle others. To those who I have hurt, please forgive me. I was wrong.

Sarcasm can be funny when it's shared with someone who is joking along. Lots of my students along the way have enjoyed trading slightly sarcastic barbs back and forth with me. We aren't being mean, just silly. If a student heads out to the restroom and I tell them not to get lost, it's fun when they pretend to look around puzzled and ask where they are. What I had to learn very early on in my career was that some students either don't understand sarcasm or don't think it's funny. I remember a student who looked right at me clearly puzzled and carefully explained that the restroom was right around the corner and that they knew where it was.

Here's what I understand though. There's a difference between finding something funny and experiencing Joy. It's possible for someone to think a joke is funny and laugh without really having a whole lot of Joy. Joy is incredible when shared. Fun can leave you empty inside sometimes. Fun is based upon what is happening at that time. Joy is based on how you feel as you live your life in the day to day.

When writing this, I thought of several episodes that I had thought were incredibly funny then and after. I have and am sharing some of them with you. Yet, when I was thinking about them in this context, I realized that there had been times when I had made someone feel bad or stupid. It gave me a whole new outlook on the events. I was having fun at the expense of others.

I think I'll stick to sharing humor with others and feeling the Joy.

• LIFE LESSON 10 •

Break Out of the Rut

When I was young, I could be a real creature of habit. Every morning, I would get up and have two pieces of peanut butter toast and a glass of milk. I was the dishwasher, so I would hold the toast on my one palm to avoid dirtying a dish and sit reading the funnies while munching away.

My dad thought it was pretty funny that I felt I had to live in a routine and he encouraged me to break the habit so I could be free to eat in other ways. I saw no reason whatsoever to do so.

One morning, I got my breakfast ready and went to get the paper off the couch where Dad had left it. The funnies were gone. Simply not there. Dad acted totally innocent when I asked him for them but I knew he had hidden them. It took a little cajoling to get them back. "Pppllleeeassseee" was not the way to get anything from my dad, so I didn't even try that tactic. It took a little conversation about being stuck in the rut, of feeling like I couldn't eat unless I had the bread effectively blocking one hand and the comic strips of the day in the other. Then he handed me the funnies.

The next day, they were gone again. When I asked where they were, Dad pointed me to the newspaper pile. Dad, as the town's biology teacher and environmentalist started an early recycling program for paper. The truck came once a month, so the stack of paper would pile in a corner of the rec room until it could be taken. Somewhere in that stack were my funnies and my toast was in the way in the search. I had to go set it down in the kitchen and start looking. As I began to look, I realized that it was worse than I thought. He had taken all of the funny sections from that month and put them all together in the middle of the pile so that I would have to dig down and then look at all of the dates on each one to find the right one. Talk about your needle in a haystack. I finally did find it but my toast was a bit chilled by that time.

On day three, I got up early and waited to run to the door to get to the paper first. I was so excited when I beat him to it. I know it wouldn't happen today but we had asked the paper person (who was my best friend's brother) to throw it in the side door. I got to that door quickly and snatched that paper up before Dad could do anything. I carried the paper with me, made my toast, and happily sat down to read my favorites while I ate. The first cartoon seemed like I had read it before, then the second, and then the third. I glanced up at the date and realized that I was rereading yesterday's funnies. Turns out that Dad had had gone out the front door, met the paper carrier, exchanged the comics, and then ran to throw it in the side door before I could get there. I never saw him, just the paper flying in.

The final day, day four, I ran to the paper and opened it to pull out a comic section with the right date on top! When I started reading, though, it struck me that the paper didn't feel quite right and that the funnies were yesterday's. Dad had carefully cut the funnies from the day before and gently glued them around the edges over today's. Seriously?

The problem wasn't that Dad was messing with the funnies. That itself was pretty funny. It's that he was messing with my need to do everything the same way all the time. I had lots of "have to" habits. For one, I counted my steps to school, kicking a tiny rock that I hid in both places and then kicked the other direction. It really slowed me down. My comfort was found in having this routine that couldn't be broken. It's the last part of the sentence that's the key. It's okay to have a routine, but this is real life. Is my security found in having everything the same every day in a changing world? Not a good thing to hang onto.

Some types of routine are amazingly helpful to living our lives. When I'm explaining to new keyboardists at school why they need to learn the correct keys for each respective finger, in order to learn to type faster, I talk to them about how they learned to tie their shoes. I ask them if they ever have to think about how to do it anymore. None of these young third and fourth graders ever say yes. They also don't need to think about brushing their teeth or how to hold their fork. They've learned how to brush their teeth and hair. All of these took thought at first, even if we don't think about them now. We've developed a routine of doing them and we just do. Typing is the same in that if we learn how to do it, our fingers will generally go to the correct keys and we can go faster. This is the way it should be.

So routine is our human default. It makes us move through life faster so that we can do more than just the daily needs. It's when we get stuck in that default that it becomes a problem. Sometimes habits become, not conveniences, but must-do's that make us anxious if we miss them. Usually over things that aren't really making our life more convenient at all. When we start to make everything a routine or add routines that we don't need to accomplish goals in life, then we don't get to do the new, the different, the adventurous of life. We may feel comfortable but are we enjoying life?

My mom's parents lived for adventure. They would be sitting there and my Grandpa would let them know that they were going out and in five minutes everyone would be in the car ready to go. Often, they were trying some new taste for dinner but who knew it was coming? My grandma believed that life was an education in itself. When Admiral Byrd took delivery of the incredible Snow Cruiser machine that he used to explore the Antarctic, he took it on a parade from where he got the tires for it in Akron, throughout the Cleveland area. Grandma determined the parade route and then ran to school to pick up Mom and Uncle Ron. They drove to a great spot to see the paraded machine. It was huge, with tires far larger than any of the people there. It moved slowly down the street with Admiral Byrd walking by its side. They were wowed! Then Grandma raced them back to the car and drove them a few miles away to another spot on the parade route so that they could see it again. She wanted them to remember it and it worked. It wasn't what they did everyday but what an incredible time. Grandma also took them outside onto the lawn chairs in the back yard to stay up all night and watch meteor showers. Years later, she would stay up late with my sister and I watching those shooting stars on warm August nights and we learned about comets and stars and so much more. Then we'd play games all night and sleep in late. Sure couldn't do that every night and day, but I loved being at Grandma's.

It was precisely because it wasn't the norm that it was even more fun. It would have been a blast anyway but that thrill of something different was like the first ride on that little old wooden roller coaster at the local amusement park. It's because we have routines in our daily lives that we have both the time to have the outside adventure and the thrill of something different than the ordinary.

There are those on the opposite end of this spectrum. Life is all about escapades, and they develop few habits beyond the basics of shoe tying and teeth brushing. The difficulty lies in accomplishing the needs of each day—how to be able to live with and work with others in a successful way. There are no ruts in their life but that can make it hard for them to follow a path that actually accomplishes everything that needs to get done in a day. I know because there have been times when I have blissfully broken out of the habits and jumped into all sorts of fun activities. Nothing harmful, just busy. Places to go, people to see, things to do, food to try, impromptu walks to take through sudden spring rains or piles of fall leaves.

The more that gets added, the less time I have to do those things that make life simpler in the long run. My work email is caught up but did I miss anything in my personal email in the last two-three days? Ok, I'll get to that stack of laundry tomorrow but I sure wish I had _____ (fill in the blank with an article of clothing for you—for me it's usually a favorite pair of jeans) to wear today. Yow, why did I eat that because that's just not settling well, and I wish I had just a couple more hours of sleep.

What dichotomous creatures we humans are. We find both a need and a Joy in the day-to-day habits that give us comfort, and an excitement in the realm outside those habits. The problem, of course, is always in the balance of these. I'm not advocating a caffeine habit to counteract your missing sleep, while staying up all night playing video games. That's not a balance. It's playing both ends against the middle. But keeping habits going that keep your life in order, while still being able to have both some planned and some spontaneous activities, that's a balance that can work.

This takes thought. Literally, I had to think through why I HAD to hold the peanut butter toast in one hand while reading the funnies in the other. I mean, was the sky going to fall on my head if I didn't do that? Would my family stop loving me? On the other hand, how bad is it if I cut something off my social calendar this month in favor of a cup of chamomile tea and a little extra sleep? Or if I ask my friend if we can meet for a nice long walk so we can do both our exercise and catch up at the same time? So I think, why on earth do I let myself get stuck in either extreme? Well, because I'm only human and that's what humans tend to do. But I have the capacity to analyze what I'm doing and realize I'm making things tough for myself.

In the process, I decided at some point to intentionally

break every habit that was actually more of a hindrance than a help. Of course it felt uncomfortable and weird but refreshing and freeing. I stopped taking exactly two steps in each sidewalk block, and (okay, usually) not counting my steps. Each time I found myself doing something because I HAD to, I decided not to, until I found out I could do without them. It was okay to ask for help on this. Nearly everyone I know has their own habitual behaviors. I let some know, hey, I'm working on this, keep encouraging me not to…do whatever. And they did—just like my dad did when I was little.

So now I use a plate for my peanut butter toast in the morning while I'm reading my funnies. Yet when I'm on the school overnight trips at my nut-free school, I can eat the cereal in the morning with the students and then get to the funnies when I get home later in the day. I know that the sky won't fall on my head even if I don't get to them.

And I have the Joy of adventures along the way.

• LIFE LESSON 11 •

The Pumpkin Pie Spice on My Salad

I t started many years ago when I was in college and it morphed from there. I didn't start out thinking I would try something new and different. It just…happened.

I was out on a date with someone I had been going out with for a few months. We generally got along extremely well and he was a nice guy. I have no explanation for why he was in such a mood that evening, I only know the evening turned into a disaster. I probably should have asked for an explanation later so I didn't still wonder.

He took me to a very nice restaurant, nicer than we college students frequented. I was looking forward to a wonderful evening. That only lasted through ordering our meal. Right after the waiter walked away, the argument started.

"Milk? Why did you order milk?"

Not only was I surprised by the question, but by the angry tone that accompanied it.

"I like milk." It seemed fairly obvious to me. Besides, he already knew that. It's what I always had with my meals if it was available.

"Why didn't you order a drink?"

It just got more surprising by the second. It was like, "Whaaattt?" going off in my head. What I got out was, "What are you talking about? I like milk. I've always liked milk. It's what I've always ordered when we've been out. I don't drink. You've never seen me drink. I don't like it."

His reply? "Well, you could at least order it so that no one thinks I'm out with a little child."

More outrageous by the moment. I was about twenty— old enough to order a beer if I wanted one. I just didn't know why I would want one when I didn't like it. I know I looked younger than my age, but really now…a child?

Honestly?

"You want me to order something I don't like and won't drink, to impress people I don't know and will never see again?"

Yes, that's exactly what he meant.

The next salvo he shot was even better. "And then you didn't order any dressing on your salad."

Huh? Not sure why that one was an issue. I tried to remain calm despite seething. "I don't like salad dressing."

Truth be told, I'm better at trying new things than when I was younger. Still if I try something and don't like it, then I don't like it. Eating it again because others are eating it does not change my mind. We all have different taste buds. I had tried salad with dressing when I was a kid and absolutely positively decided against it.

The fact is that I don't like vegetables. I know people who love them will tell me how different they all are and how wonderful and how I should love them. More power to those of you who feel this way—it's easier for you to eat those daily veggies to stay healthy. I need to work at it. Adding another taste I don't like, such as dressing, on to those vegetables just make it worse. Far worse.

As I look back at this newest angry outburst in the restaurant, it becomes apparent that both angry statements actually led back to the same issue, "What will people think?" He cared and I didn't.

I didn't analyze all that at the time. I was just stunned at the way the conversation was happening.

However, before an angry retort could fall from my mouth, He dropped the most challenging statement of the evening. I mean literally challenging.

"What are you going to do next to embarrass me? Put sugar on your salad?"

That's the night I found out that I *really* like sugar on my salad. I don't know how many packets I opened and poured on there but it was enough to be totally obnoxious. And I couldn't taste the vegetables. It was great. Not healthy, but delicious.

The relationship did not last. The sugar on the salad did—for years. I just put smaller amounts on.

I thought I should get kudos for finding a way to get the salad down but most just thought it was weird.

A few years back, my metabolism started slowing down along with my activity level and energy level. The obvious result was that I put on some extra weight. Now my husband and my youngest son sat me down for a conversation. They made it perfectly clear that they both love me very much and the conversation wasn't about the weight. It was about my health. You see, my family specializes in diabetes. I'm one of the few family members who doesn't have it, and even I had it during pregnancy. Doctors had told me more than once that extra weight could trigger the disease for me. My son was diagnosed at eight and he sure didn't want me to have it. Being unhealthy is not a key to Joy, nor having a disease that requires daily finger sticks and shots that could cause me far worse issues as I grow older.

They were right, of course. It's not something I want. I needed to exercise more and eat better so that I could be around for my whole family for a much longer time.

Here's where we get stuck in the process though. What should I do? I tell people I can't run very much because I've torn the cartilage in my knee twice. The first time I had surgery. The second time, they advised me not to run or do other exercise that hurt because a second surgery wouldn't be very helpful. I'm okay with that because even if I didn't have torn cartilage, running is not an activity I want to do. I never really enjoyed running even when I was a kid. I walked really fast, I swam, biked, somersaulted all the way across the longest yards, but I didn't want to run.

I think a lot of us get hung up on the idea of exercising because we think of it as getting on a treadmill and running forever, and we hate the idea. There are many people who love running like my husband and youngest and I'm really glad they do. But it sure doesn't motivate me.

I have to exercise though. I want to live a long healthy life and play on the playground with my grandchildren someday. So I had to find something I did like. That's the key. I love walking and I walk very fast. I also love swimming—one of the best places on earth is at the bottom of the pool, looking at the sunlight coming through the water. I'm not fast in the water, but I can swim for hours. So all I had to do was do what I liked. I started walking a half-hour a day right after dinner. I found lots of people out walking in the neighborhood and started walking with others and talking as we went. So I walk often. Sometimes I'll arrange to meet a friend at a park for a hike. Sometimes, I'll take off into the woods on my own and go off trail climbing over logs and jumping through leaves like a little kid again. Sometimes in winter, I'll stop and make snow angels on the high school lawn or throw a snow ball across the field just for the fun of it. Sometimes, I don't bother to look at my watch and I lose track of the time, and I just keep walking for a while. Maybe I'll stop at the library to look at the used book sale or to watch a little league game and remember when my oldest played—for just a couple minutes and then walk some more with a smile. I also have been doing races with my husband (and sometimes youngest when we're in the same city) for years now. They run, I walk but we all get to the finish line. I walk pretty fast, too, because I like it.

In summer, I'll swim for most of the afternoon at the city pool. Until my Dad passed away last year, we'd swim together. Even in his eighties, he still swam the full length of this large pool without taking a breath. I can't do it but I keep trying. As an early 60th birthday celebration, my husband took me to the ocean so I could fulfill a life-time dream of learning to surf. It was absolutely remarkable! Yes, I did actually ride a wave in, after only two hours of instruction with the help of an incredible instructor and his wife. Exercise can be an adventure!

Some of you are likely thinking that none of that sounds fun at all. That's okay. It's how I feel about running.

What would you really enjoy that involves faster movement? Racquetball? Soccer? Basketball? Rollerblading like one of my favorite superintendents? What about rock-climbing or squash, or…look around where you live and see what's there.

What about activities that accomplish something else at the same time? We don't own a snow blower, we own shovels. They work well and I think about how buying myself more years as my heart works to complete the job. We also don't own a leaf blower.

And what if I accidentally jump in that pile of leaves after they're raked? Or find myself making a few snowballs to toss across the yard? What if the great-niece and great-nephews and their friends and future grandchildren all want to play on the playground and need someone to chase them and push their swings and go down the slide with them? Play never came with an age limit.

Want to watch that show but you need to walk? March in place in front of the TV for the whole show. Exercise can be part of the Joy we have in our lives. Lots and lots of choices out there.

Back to where we started here: the diet aspect of all this. Sugar on the salad was likely not the best way to avoid becoming diabetic. So what should I do? Well the concept is the same—use what you do enjoy in order to deal with what you don't enjoy. I know that if I burn off more calories than I ingest that I will lose weight. I know that this sounds way too simplistic. I'm a teacher—I want to put everything in simple terms. And I like simple; it helps me get the idea so that I can actually incorporate it into my life.

The concept of how to improve the diet was the same basis as the exercise. What did I enjoy eating, what did I like? How could I use that to make it easier to eat the things I don't like?

So there I was at the salad bar at work, dutifully putting salad parts on my tray. I had the lettuce and cucumber and some (yuck) broccoli. There at the end of the line was a lovely tray of mixed fruit. I can't eat the citrus fruits with my Vitamin C allergy, of course. But this was cantaloupe, honeydew, and grapes. And there were bananas nearby. There didn't seem to be a spot on my tray for them. That's when it hit me. I used what I loved, to deal with what I didn't. I scooped up the fruit and dropped it right on top of my salad. It worked! Broccoli *is* better with honeydew and banana. I began to bury my vegetables in fresh fruits. Delicious and healthy!

The next real change happened a couple of years back. I was reading about healthy spices and read up on cinnamon and how good it is for you. I love cinnamon. So I did the logical and obvious: I added some to my salad. Turns out that it's pretty good on the fruit and thus on the vegetables.

Then the final stage. I reached into the cupboard one evening for the cinnamon and saw the pumpkin pie spice next to it. Yes! Not just cinnamon, but other wonderful, healthy spices. And could it make my salad taste like pumpkin pie? I had washed the fruits and vegetables, so they were wet. When I added the pumpkin pie spice and mixed it up, the water and spices mixed into a sort of glaze. It was terrific! It's at least an aromatic, tasty reminder of pumpkin pie. Well worth it. I call it the salad for salad haters.

I brought an extra jar of pumpkin pie spice to work and

I put it in a cupboard in the dining area. Before I went half time last year, I would get my lunch tray each day and put my salad/fruit on the side. Then I would pull out the spice and add it. Some eating with me would laugh, some joke, some were obviously repulsed by the idea while still polite (which is okay—it's how I feel about that horrible salad dressing they were eating). Some, though, have tried it. Not all liked it, but some did.

The point of this lesson, of course, is not that you have to try pumpkin pie spice on your salad if you prefer pumpkin pie to salad (although you can, if you're feeling adventurous). In the long run, there are several lessons here—some stronger than others, but all part of the package of living in Joy.

First of all is the understanding of your value as an individual. People talk a lot about being individuals. "Respect yourself", "Be Yourself", "Stand out from the crowd!" In reality, most feel far more secure staying in the crowd. If everyone else is doing the same thing, then we must be "right" about it. People who stand out make people uncomfortable. They make us wonder if we are doing what we should be doing. We not only end up being like other people and letting go of those things we might do on our own, we also end up pushing those around us into conformity.

So few are really happy being like everyone else, they're just afraid that they won't be happy if they are "different" from the rest.

I could have ordered a drink to just sit there while I ate so that others thought of me as a grown-up, but I would have spent the entire dinner wishing I had a milk. All to impress a roomful of strangers who didn't even know me and would never see me again. That would not have brought me Joy.

Far deeper than enjoying my meal, however, is the compromise on my beliefs. I'm about to give you a sort of lengthy description of why I don't drink. Not because I expect you to drop your beliefs about drinking, but to show that I have definite reasons for my choice. Sometimes understanding why someone makes a choice helps in accepting the fact that aren't going along with the crowd.

Despite my own safe wonderful home growing up, I had seen too many homes damaged by alcoholism growing up. I saw people who seemed like nice people when sober turn into angry scary people. I saw families torn apart. I saw people losing control of their behavior so that they appeared foolish in front of anyone who wasn't drinking. Watching people throw up at wedding receptions did not impress me either. I hate getting sick. None of it left an impression of "fun" on me. I'm not preaching abstinence to those who drink. I'm not judging my friends or relatives or anyone else who wants a beer or glass of wine. I just realized rather young that it didn't look like fun to me. When I was old enough to try a drink, I took a sip and realized I didn't like the taste—not even a little. Finally, I'm a person who wants to be in control of my own actions. I don't want anything to make me lose control. This all adds up to "This is just not me."

So I not only refrain from drinking, I also don't want to appear as if I do. It would be me saying that I think it's a good idea, when I really don't. It's going along with the crowd idea that this is a great thing for everyone to do, when for some it can be quite dangerous. We all know people who have died in accidents, others who have found out too late that the alcoholism in their family is indeed hereditary, and others who have lost the rights to see their children. It's not what I want for me. Peer pressure doesn't change that. My friends who drink respect my choice as I respect theirs. In my late twenties, I was at a dinner party when someone at the table said that they had never seen me drink. I told them that I just didn't like it. Their reply was, "I don't either. I just do it because everyone else does." He was someone I knew well enough to be able to reply, "You're twenty-seven years old. When are you going to outgrow that?"

So whatever your choice here, let it be your choice. If you have a good time having a beer or two with your friends or whether you don't like it, make your decision based upon what you like, want, and believe—not on some group of people who may be influenced by others.

The same is true, of course, for everything that comes up as, "Well, everyone else is doing it." Negative peer pressure can push someone to dangerous, unhealthy, or destructive activities. I have never seen true Joy in any of this. There may be laughter, but it's a fleeting feeling that soon flickers and fades as the crowd disperses into the real world leaving nothing real or lasting.

Just as destructive, while far more hidden, is the loss of self in the collective. When I was in high school in the 70's, young women were encouraged to become teachers, nurses, secretaries, or homemakers. These were the choices. Men had a lot more choices, but they also had limits. They could be doctors, but not nurses. They could be teachers, but not in elementary school. There were those of both genders who didn't listen to culture and who formed a path for others to follow. Yet, it makes one wonder how many scientists, mathematicians, engineers, writers, artists, musicians, doctors, and others were lost who could have changed the world. How many people have lived their entire adult life working at jobs that brought them no Joy or happiness because they were following the societal norms rather than staying true to themselves? How many still are?

What about your spare time? What is the newest "gotta do" activity that "everyone" is doing? Do you enjoy it? Is there something else you'd rather do despite how others feel about it? I'm likely stepping on toes with this one—just don't take it personally if I disagree with you. I'm not taking it personally that you disagree with me.

Back in the early 80's, I did a popular exercise class program set to music. I'm musically inept but it was fun exercise and I enjoyed it. Since then, I've seen many an exercise activity come and go as the "in" way to keep fit.

Some of it more fun for me than others. A long, fast walk in a race on a Saturday morning for charity? Count me in! Exercise video on TV while trying to balance on a large inflatable ball? Good for many, not so much fun for me. Basketball game with friends? Yes! Yoga? No.

It's that last one that tends to upset people. They wouldn't mind if I turned it down because I didn't enjoy that type of exercise, even if they don't understand why anyone wouldn't enjoy it. But it's not the exercise that keeps me away. I tend to study things before I get involved. When I studied what yoga was about, I found that it has a religious basis. That's fine. It's just not my religion. It's not popular to say that you don't want to do something because it's outside of your religion.

People see it as intolerant. In truth, it is real tolerance. If others try to force me to give up my beliefs, and agree that all people should believe that all beliefs are essentially the same, we all lose our beliefs in the sameness. If I truly believe in my faith, why should I give it up for some generic, one-size-fits-all system where all religions are merely blended into one big idea that everything is identical? One's religion becomes a way to conform with the crowd, instead of a choice based upon the individual's conscience. This is disrespectful and intolerant to everyone. It is also disrespectful and intolerant to suggest that all people take part in the religious activities of all faiths even if they don't share the belief system. I didn't require my friend to celebrate Easter this year, any more than she is requiring Rosh Hashanah of me. I've never asked a Muslim student to stop fasting during Ramadan because I'm eating then. I would never encourage either to eat my favorite meat, pork chops. It would be disrespectful of their beliefs. So is pushing me to do yoga when I have politely said no. True tolerance and respect is when we believe that all people of all faiths, and those who have no faith, are allowed to live by their beliefs. Intolerance brings anger and frustration instead of Joy.

Many tell me that yoga is just exercise without a spiritual basis and many enjoy it. They have the right to have that basis for their exercise, and there is no need to argue with them. The point is that we have the right attitude in our disagreement. Can we respect each other in the process? Do we have the right to disagree?

The answer is that often people disagree with me about not doing the yoga. I have never told any of them that they can't do yoga. I've simply demurred from attending myself. The reactions have varied greatly. Most are fine with it but some have been very angry. It doesn't matter. I need to never do anything because "everyone else is doing it." I need to be true to my beliefs or I will end up being unhappy. I'm not sure why anyone else would be happy in trying to force me to do something I don't agree with, any more than I could ever find happiness in forcing them into going against themselves.

The truth is that you don't need to go against what you believe, or like, or dislike, or enjoy, or your goals and dreams in life because of others. Be you, even when the pressure is on.

So, in this multi-purpose chapter we have covered a myriad array of topics. General health, exercise, diet, alcohol use, nonconformity to the crowd, and the tolerance to allow us to make our decisions based upon our beliefs. Isn't that how life is? We tend to compartmentalize and categorize and try to separate out everything into little sound bits. Sometimes that works, and explains why this book is made of separate chapters. More often than not, however, the pieces of our lives are all connected into the whole. They relate to each other in ways that will not work as well when separated. We really do need to look at the whole and relate it and figure out where we stand in all of that, in order to be our best selves.

And to live a joyful life.

• LIFE LESSON 12 •
It Only Takes a Moment

I may have mentioned that I LOVE basketball. I'll watch other sports sometimes, particularly if Cleveland is playing. I'll cheer whether it's the Indians, or the Browns, or the Cavs. If you offer me a choice of tickets though, I'm taking the Cavs.

It isn't just the pros that I watch. I also thoroughly enjoy college games. When I was in my early twenties I stayed up almost all night for the longest Division 1 college game ever played. I was cheering for Cincinnati and thrilled to see them win by two in the seventh overtime. As exhausted as I was the next day, I was happy. March Madness (the national college tournament for you non-basketball fans) is a time when my family all sits down and fills out family brackets to see who gets the most games correct. I love those bragging rights in the years I win! I love watching the games even more. Isn't it great that my school always has spring break during some of those games?

All of this to explain how I got the greatest summer job EVER back in the early 80's.

I didn't make a lot of money my first few years of teaching, so I worked for a temporary agency for the first few summers. I moved to North Carolina in June, right after school let out and went straight to the agencies to get working. I'm grateful that my mom had made me take typing in high school (Thanks, Mom! You helped me prepare for adulthood in a million ways—you're the best!), I went in and took the tests to show that I could type and alphabetize files and write letters, etc.

Now, some people don't enjoy temporary work but for me it worked really well. I knew if I didn't particularly like a position that I wouldn't be there for long (pulling staples out of stacks of papers one day for eight hours or copying 275 copies of a large document at another place were about the least fun. But they were…temporary). Trust me, I had some comparatives. I had worked my way into and through college by trying a wide variety of jobs: waitressing (I bet I broke a record for the number of pennies earned in one night), hostessing (I was polite to those being mean to me, but it was a little tough gritting my teeth so much), store work (long before the days of bar code scanners), and factory work (making drill bits with a machine that overheated daily and threw hot silver on me). I respect and admire people who do these jobs—I just found out that I wasn't any good at them. So finding the temporary work was really helpful for me. I liked the variety and the work, and met many interesting and diverse people. I was helping companies that had a rush project or who were temporarily short-handed because of vacations or a gap between someone leaving and someone coming and I liked doing that.

Which brings me inevitably back to basketball. One day a call came through asking if I would work for Duke's basketball office. A secretary had left and the new one couldn't start for a week.

Would I work for Coach K. at Duke for a week? How quickly could I say YES! Basketball fans are already drooling. For the rest of you, Coach Mike Krzyzewski is a legend. He's been the head coach for this high-ranking team since 1980. Although only in his third year, when I walked in, he was already known as one of the very best—an honor he richly deserved. I found myself unusually nervous that first morning.

I should preface the next part with a small caveat that explains how wonderful this job turned out to be. Although most places were absolutely thrilled to have the extra set of hands an extra worker provides, that's not always true. One manager absolutely needed extra help, but didn't believe that he could trust a temporary worker with more than pulling staples. He stopped me to ask if I was capable of understanding what they were doing. The tone indicated that no answer I gave would prove that I had any ability to think at all.

At another job, I discovered an issue with the computer system's dating, but was told by a member of the tech department that I was just a temp and what did I know about computers anyway. I told him that I did understand what the date was and that what the computer was putting as the date in saved documents was not it. And since all documents with old dates were going to be purged in a couple of days, I thought it might be an issue. For those who only know modern servers, the older servers didn't have large capacities. Older documents needed to be reopened once a month so that they got a newer date stamp or off they went. It didn't take a tech whiz to understand that the time stamp on our documents being off could be a real problem. I learned from it though. As an instructional technologist, I want to be sure that I don't start with an assumption about what teachers and students know or don't know about the computers.

It amazes me that our perception of people is so based upon the job they are in. I am the same person when teaching but that gets respect. Shouldn't everyone be getting respect for doing their jobs no matter what their jobs are? That's not as much of a digression as it might seem. Because at Duke, I was treated with respect.

I walked into the incredible gym where the Duke Blue Devils play their home games, stunned and amazed that I was there. I was greeted warmly at the basketball office and shown my desk with great kindness, consideration, and gratitude that I was there to help. I got right to work, sorting out the letters from all of the high school students who were requesting to play for Duke. In the midst of this, players were coming in. They all introduced themselves. It was actually pretty funny, because my 5'3" inch frame sitting at a desk had to reach my arm up really, really high in order to shake hands when those long arms stretched down.

Work places follow those at the helm. This office was being run by a man who showed kindness and respect to all who came in. It's not that he wasn't in charge—Coach K. knows how to lead, how to set parameters, how to get things done. All of us there returned his respect with respect. During that week, I found him to be a joy to work for. We all worked together for this team and this coach. I also got to meet his wife and his oldest daughter (the rest of his family came later), who were just as personable. It was a dream job.

Thursday night my phone rang and it was my supervisor at the temp agency. She wanted to let me know that I wouldn't be needed on Friday. I was broken-hearted. My immediate question was whether I had done something wrong. The answer is what brings about this whole chapter.

My supervisor said, "Oh, no. Coach K. wanted to make sure you didn't think that. His new secretary was just able to start a day early. He wanted me to tell you, so that you didn't think you had done anything wrong. He was actually very pleased with your work."

I wanted to cry.

We are taught in our society early about class separation. It's why people think that restaurant workers, factory workers, and temp workers just aren't as valuable. It's not true—but truth doesn't always change the perception of reality.

Fortunately, not all follow the crowd on this one.

Coach K. did not owe me any explanation. This was his office, his work, his time. He did something incredible. He took a moment, a sliver of his valuable time, to reassure a temp worker who had been in his office only four days. That moment meant a great deal to me. We all need that reassurance that we matter, that we have value, that we are noticed in life. In one small moment, this great coach gave that to me.

As we go rushing through life, how many opportunities do we have to give those small moments to someone else? How many times do we see someone and have the chance to say or do something reassuring, kind, or encouraging? Today, it's easier than ever before. We can use text, email, chat, and a million other electronic ways of communication to drop that quick word of reassurance. We can do the old-fashioned drop off a quick little gift or send a letter. We can open our phone and have something sent over to someone anywhere in the world. We can still give a quick hug to those who need it, a smile, a pat on the arm. We can give take-home or take-out to the hungry person on the street or we can drop food off at the homeless shelter.

How do I count the ways?

It isn't about class status ultimately. In this case, it just made the encouraging word less likely. It's about human. What can we do when we encounter other humans to make their day?

First, see all people as humans.

When I used to do volunteer ministry at the juvenile detention center, I encountered kids who had spent their lives short of reassurance that they were human, valuable, real, loved. When parents are so wrapped up in themselves and their problems, it's hard to reassure the kids. Many of the parents were on drugs or alcoholic, most had serious financial difficulties with little or no job prospects or were working as many hours a week as they could get in just to survive. Both, the kids and the parents, are humans living in tough situations and often not surviving well. Many of the kids had been abused by people who had been abused by people who had been…

Those of us who volunteered went in with the thought that these young human beings needed to be cared for and needed to find out that they were worth it. We went in to talk and listen and develop relationships where we could find ways to validate them. The kids responded to the love and respect. One young lady had just gotten there and was sitting sobbing when we walked in. When we left, she was hugging us and smiling with joy and held the belief that she could help other girls there. When we returned in two weeks, she was still smiling and rapidly told us how she had been telling the other girls that they too could get through it all.

It was often easier for me to see the kids as human than their parents. I had to work on that. There is no helping someone based on hatred or even disinterest. The issues we have in our society will never be solved by anger, hatred, judgment, resentment, or a host of other spiteful and negative motivations. They will only perpetuate the problems. Only when we see people as human, can we find ways to reach out and help them in any meaningful way. It is the dehumanizing of people that has made the most horrific annuls of mankind happen. The Holocaust, slavery, the current genocides in the Sudan are unfortunately only some of the worst examples of this. Those who dehumanized the people they ruthlessly enslaved, tortured, and murdered had lost their own humanity. Otherwise they could not have committed the atrocities upon others. We need to be extremely cautious about how we allow dehumanization in our own attitudes towards others and in our society and culture before it leads to far worse.

I need to retain my humanity and see these struggling parents as humans who need help as much and sometimes more than their children.

This all starts on a much smaller level. "People who __

are __" It often starts with hearing others make those little statements and just agreeing on auto-pilot based upon things you may have in common with the speaker. Political affiliation, race, gender, religious beliefs, nationality, family thought, and down to the minute details such as rural or city-dweller. Of course, you may really agree with many things said but do you take the time to think about what you are hearing and figure out why you agree?

Many years ago, I moved out of state and went to a church that seemed like a great place. I really had a great experience there. However, as I was heading out towards my car, I overheard a conversation where a man was saying that he was really glad that when a murderer had been killed in a raid, that his little daughter had been killed, too. The hearers agreed with this. It was a "Yeah, that will show him!" type of conversation. I know that some agreed because they agree, but I wonder how many just went along with the statement because the speaker was a leader in the church and they figured he knew. I had no way to reconcile it with my religious beliefs at all. Rejoicing in the death of that innocent child? I decided to start the church hunt again.

When I was in third grade, the Presidential election between Lyndon Johnson and Barry Goldwater took place. (I'll save you the trouble, I was born in 1956.) As we were studying this process, I came home and went straight to my parents with a question. "Are we Democrats or Republicans?" My parents explained that they could tell me what they usually voted, but that it didn't matter in terms of my future votes. They told me that I was too young to make that decision but that as I got older, I would need to check out what each political party believed and more importantly, what each candidate believed. I could then figure out which candidate I agreed with most and make a decision. I listened intently and then told them that I thought I'd probably pick Republican because I'd rather be an elephant than a donkey. They didn't think that was the way to pick either but fuller explanations of looking at issues and solutions, viewpoints, and individual candidates needed to wait until I was a little older. I'm not either animal actually—I vote per candidate per office. But I needed to learn to judge based on facts.

The first Presidential election I could vote in was the 1976 contest between Jimmy Carter and Gerald Ford. As people started announcing their candidacies, I heard a knock on my Kent State dorm door. I opened it to find a huge poster of a man's face in front of me with a hand holding the top and the bottom. Behind the poster I heard an unknown voice ask, "Isn't that a great smile?" I returned question for question, "Who is it?"

"Jimmy Carter. He's running for President, and you should vote for him." the voice replied. I asked the obvious next question—obvious to me at least. "Where does he stand on some of the main issues?"

You may not believe the answer any more than I did.

"I don't know, but doesn't he have a great smile?"

I'm thinking he wasn't thinking. He was following those who had given him the poster and sent him out, but he didn't have details to even think about. For me, it wasn't about the candidate's smile, or someone telling me to vote for someone they believed in, or a candidate's name, or a host of other reasons I've heard—it was about what they would do or not do as President.

Which makes the current political arena particularly distressing for me. It doesn't matter to me which party you belong to or if you are Independent. What I'm hearing now, however, is the most hate-filled rhetoric running back and forth. Both sides are vilifying the other to the point where it is becoming impossible to find a middle ground to accomplish anything at all. Life is tough for a lot of people right now and when they need something done to help them they find impasses and pointing fingers from those elected to solve the problems. "Of course you're not getting helped because THEY aren't helping you."

To all our elected officials who are reading this, I recommend that you read President Kennedy's book *Profiles in Courage* – particularly the chapter on Edmund G. Ross who was condemned by his party and lost his re-election when he voted to acquit Andrew Johnson. I think today things are different, however, in that many of us would like to re-elect those who think for themselves.

I'm not trying to be offensive to anyone in any party. Quite the contrary. I believe in a system where you can have disagreeing parties and your own opinion, as to which one you want to align. I'm also not digressing as much as it seems. I am instead giving specific examples of how dehumanization works. Vilifying political opponents dehumanizes them and you hear the results in the speech of the people following the politician spewing the angry rhetoric. It's not the political system or either party that I'm against here. I'm against the loss of respect for people who disagree with us.

Let's see if I can make the second point a bit more concise (no promises though).

The second point is related to the first: Give up the preconceived notions you have about those around you. Stereotypes dehumanize even without rhetoric.

People are far too complex for preconceived notions to work.

Back in the early 1980's when I was living far from my family, the post office was just part of my routine. There were no computers, no internet, no cell phones, and long distance phone calls were a bit expensive to use as a continual means of communication. We wrote letters and we mailed them.

I made friends with the woman who worked at my local post office. We were about the same age and had a lot of in common. When there were no lines we would chat and laugh and just enjoy the friendship. The fact that she was black and I was white was just totally irrelevant in any way.

One day, there was a very long line and I waited a bit. I'm obviously a pretty sociable person, so I struck up little conversations with those around me as we inched forward.

However, I was stunned by a comment from the woman behind me. She made one of the most racist remarks I've ever heard about my friend at the counter, indicating that my friend who she called a name that I wouldn't repeat here or anywhere, should be quiet and not talk to people so we could get up there. That took impatience to levels I had never dreamed. I looked at her for a moment and then simply turned my back on her. She obviously assumed that since I was white that I agreed with her.

A couple of minutes later I got to the counter and leaned over to give my friend a hug and a warm greeting. I then turned to look at the woman behind me who was startled and shocked. I told her that her remark was uncalled for and wrong. She had stereotyped both of us with her ideas of what it is to be black or white. It is unlikely, unfortunately, that it affected her racist ideology, but I hope it affected her preconceived notions enough that at some point she could reconsider those beliefs.

Respecting someone as human doesn't mean that we have to just agree with them. Sometimes we take our stand on what we believe is right or wrong. We just do so in a way that doesn't make us wrong. Cursing her and calling her names would have been me dehumanizing. I don't want to go there. The civil rights movement proved that standing up for what is right can be done in a way that doesn't make the one standing up for it wrong.

After forty years of teaching, I wish I could say that those stereotypes have gone away.

Carol is a very smart woman. Back in school, she was an excellent student. She loves opera, ballet, classical music, history, reading; did drama and choir; is a tremendous accounts manager when math was her "weakest" subject in school. She is also the wittiest person I know. Her natural hair color? Blonde, very blonde. Countless times, men aimed dumb blonde jokes at her. When we were at some event as young adults, I watched her try a couple of times, nicely, to stop the remarks that one man was making. He was on a roll and kept on going joke after joke while totally ignoring her requests to stop. I kept quiet, waiting. Trust me, Carol does not need my help in these matters. Finally, she gently patted the top of his head, just above the forehead where his hair had receded quite a bit.

She remarked, "Okay, I admit it. It's my blonde hair that makes me stupid. What's responsible for you?" It took him a moment to get it. He started with "Huh?" and ended with "Wait, are you insulting me?" She admitted it of course.

Since she now had his attention, she took a moment to admonish him for being rude and insulting and stereotyping her based on her hair color. He took the admonishment, too. It's good to know when you've crossed the line and can admit it.

Do most people know that they are making jokes based on stereotypes they may not entirely believe? Sure. On the other hand, most make the jokes because they have some kernel of belief in them and some laugh because they wholeheartedly believe them.

The problem intensifies because, in those beliefs, people feel like they have to act out those stereotypes. "I am __ so I have to __." Doing this reinforces the stereotype to everyone. Do we act certain ways because of our race or gender or ethnicity or social class? Does any of our behaviors go counter to who we really are? That doesn't sound like winning to me.

How many stereotypes do we carry and believe, and how does that affect how we treat others and how we act for ourselves? It's something we all need to examine ourselves for, so that we can guard against negative reactions toward others.

If I proclaim right now that I am a Christian, does that after twelve chapters of this book affect your picture of who I am and what I'm like? If you are not a Christian does it make you believe that I'm an awful, hateful, hypocritical, stupid person? If you are a Christian, does it make you automatically accept what I say? Neither should happen.

People are more complex than that and there is so much you don't know about who I am.

I'm a little past middle-aged, short, with long, light brown hair with a little gray, and blue eyes. I am generally extremely energetic and all without caffeine. I'm thrilled that after thirty-six years of teaching I get to work part-time (afternoons only) so that I can start school later. I'm more of a night person than a morning person. I love peanut butter sandwiches and soy bars. There is nothing like a great meal of pork chops and mashed potatoes. I love chocolate! Yet I eat healthy, generally speaking, and do all I can to stay healthy. I have an incredible family of several generations— one above me and a couple below me. I love sudoku and reading the comics with my breakfast.

I love technology but only recently got a Facebook page and Instagram. I love walking in the sun—and in the rain and the snow. If I'm at a beach, and that's where I'd like to be, I'm in the water swimming and jumping through the waves and laughing. I learned how to surf at fifty-nine. I enjoy classical music, as well as contemporary music that avoids all the language that needs to be bleeped. I used to promote some of the hard rock Christian bands in our area and I still love to get in the front rows of concerts and dance and jump and clap and cheer. A few years ago, I danced for over seven hours at a concert, only to find out a couple of days later that the foot I had hurt in a car accident days earlier was actually broken. Oops.

Charles Dickens is my favorite author. I'm not really into Shakespeare. I think it's a blast to play on the playground with my great-niece and why can't I go down the slide or swing at my age? No reason I know of. I am left-brained and right-brained, and ambidextrous. I love doing number games and puzzles by myself, and family game nights with my family. I love winning and watching other people win. I love writing and other creative endeavors as much as I love figuring out a new computer software. I have zero musical or artistic ability, and I'm okay with that. I love non-harmful practical jokes. I'm an open book on many aspects of my life, but I'm still a pretty private person in many ways. I'm outgoing and sociable, but I'm not someone who wants to be hospitable and open my home to others and entertain. I love public speaking and being in front of others. Spiders and snakes I love; normal fears are not my fears. My biggest fear was always the fear of heights—which I was able to get over because I didn't want to live afraid.

Why bother telling you all of this? This is just showing what some might think are contradictions, but they are actually not. This is part of the complexity of being human.

To decide who someone is based upon one factor is rather limiting.

That's not to say that factors don't have any affect upon us. There are factors that we choose and factors we don't choose, all which different in depth. For example, I didn't choose to be white; I just am. It has made some difference in how others view me and treat me but no effect on how I choose to live my life. On the other hand, I chose to become a Christian in 1995 after years of investigating different religions and ideas because I came to believe that it is true. This does affect how I behave as I live out my beliefs. A major example would be that my faith tells me that all human beings have value and all human beings are to be loved and respected. This is true whether or not we agree on even the basics in life. No differences in politics, religion, race, class status, nationality, gender, economic status, or anything else can ever change this truth for me. It doesn't mean that I will agree with everyone on everything, quite the contrary, I couldn't possibly do so and still have my own beliefs. It means that I care about others whether I agree with them or not. The question is not whether I will care, the question is whether others will accept me as human and care back, even if they think I'm totally wrong.

My faith calls me not to judge others, but to love them and respect them. It calls me to live, not in anger and walking around morose, but in Joy.

Once a little Orthodox Jewish boy at an orthodox school where I was teaching looked up at me and asked why I hated him. My heart broke. I told him I didn't hate him at all, that I thought he was wonderful. He told me that he had been told that everyone like me hated him. I told him that there were sometimes people who go to church, but who don't really believe any of it, but that people who really believe it, love him and don't hate him or anyone else. He understood that and accepted it. He had learned a stereotype based upon those who claim faith but are not living it.

I think I'll just skip the stereotypes about me and others. There is no Joy in trying to live up to stereotypes or projecting them on others. There is no Joy in not being a complete, complex person, but being some two-dimensional figure who just follows the crowd even when they are wrong. There is no Joy in barriers. There is a great deal of Joy in continuing to be who we are while still interacting with others.

So we go back to the reason we started all this.

Look at all around you as human while you go through each day trying to live joyfully. Then take the next step. Taking a moment, here and there to acknowledge that humanity in someone around us, and to do something or say something to lift them up. Our lives have many moments. How many of them can we spend simply caring about others and letting them know they are cared for? You'll be amazed at the Joy that it brings to others and you.

Go Duke!

And Thank You, Coach K.! It's a moment I'm sure you don't remember but that I will not forget.

• LIFE LESSON 13 •
The "Lucky" Lesson

I'm home for a "cold" day today from school. It's below freezing and not a good idea to have students at bus stops if they can get frostbite within the first five minutes—so I'm glad we're home. We'll be home tomorrow as well. While I love my job, my reaction is, "Yes!" every time the phone rings to say stay home.

Sometimes the students don't realize that the teachers like snow days (or other surprise stay home days) as much as the kids. They forget that most of us are really still kids at heart.

At my school, when the meteorologists start predicting snow days, there's a belief that if you say the words "snow day" that you have jinxed it and it won't happen. Yesterday at church, a couple of kids told me what kids at their school do. One said that they have to wear their pajamas backwards the night before. Another said that others tape a penny to the wall. It cracked me up.

I asked her how on earth a penny taped to a wall could possibly affect the wind currents bringing the snow.

Maybe it's because my father retired from being a science teacher after sixty-six years. I grew up learning cause and effect. He also taught me magic tricks, explaining how they work. I learned about how the great magician, Harry Houdini, spent his life debunking those who claimed to be doing something supernatural when they were really doing magic tricks. Another great magician, Harry Blackstone, Jr., has followed in Mr. Houdini's footsteps. Neither would have minded if the people they debunked said they were magicians doing tricks—it was the deception that they could do something superhuman that bothered both. Learning about this, I am skeptical about anything that claims weird cause and effects.

I had a friend in high school who opened the morning paper and offered me advice based on my birthday. The first day, she read this, "Be nice to your friends today." I assured her that I would be nice to her that day, but added that I would be glad to slap her the next day if I didn't need to be nice every day. No, I didn't hit her the next day, or any day. The next day, she read, "Avoid accidents today." I replied, "Sure, today I'll avoid accidents. Tomorrow I'll walk in front of a truck." The third day she didn't read anything to me. I had laughingly let her know that I generally tried to follow good advice, but that I don't need my advice from a column in the newspaper. She didn't stick to having the paper tell her how to live either.

I had another friend who lived on a street where the local funeral parlor sat on the corner. One Friday in junior high, I walked home with her after school to have a typical sleepover with lots of pizza and candy. I walked along with her as she took the shortcut through the parking lot of that funeral home. Her mom took that corner in her car in time to see us cut through and she was extremely upset when we got to the house. She confronted us about cutting through and then asked her daughter, "You didn't breathe while walking through that parking lot, did you? Because if you breathed going through there, you'll be the next one in that funeral home." Trust me, it was really hard not to laugh and risk offending her sweet mom when my friend answered, "Mother, if I don't breathe going through there, I will surely be the next one in there." It's been over forty years, and thankfully, she is still breathing.

In what or who do you put your trust? Who do you believe? How do you decide what to do in life and what will happen to you in life?

Whatever or whoever you trust has power over your life. You want to choose carefully then.

Someone once got me a bamboo plant as a gift. It was a beautiful little plant and I set it on my desk at work and tried hard to keep it alive. Generally you can assume that most plants I get will have a very short life span. I never seemed to get the right amount of water, sunshine, whatever they need. Anyway, another teacher came in to my room and exclaimed, "Wow, great bamboo plant, it's good luck, especially if it has—" At that point she was leaning over it counting shoots and she looked up shocked and said, "Uh-oh!" It was hysterical. So I asked her, "Do you think that my life is controlled by how many shoots that plant on my desk has?" She thought for a moment and agreed with me that it really wasn't.

I am not condemning you or making fun of you if you have superstitions. I am suggesting since you are reading a book on living joyfully, that they are unlikely to lead you to Joy. Worrying about whether you've done everything correctly to make sure that you get lucky in life is not a recipe for peace and happiness.

One presidential election year, before computers in schools, I got some large poster boards for my class to study the process. First, they got newspapers and started studying the issues that were being discussed. On one poster board the students started listing the different issues across the top and then split the page below them to write in the different viewpoints on those issues. Then, they created their own sheets where they rank-ordered those issues from those they thought were the most important to their least important. Then, they picked which side they were agreed with most for each. The second poster board was used to list the presidential candidates down the left side and the issues across the top so that they could fill in the candidates' viewpoints on each. Finally, they decided individually which candidate matched their viewpoints the best.

As students presented what they had found out about the different sides of the issues, one student found herself agreeing with everything being presented—first one side and then the other. On about the third issue she asked me in frustration what I believed. She said, "Just tell me which one to choose." I asked her how that would help her when she was older. My opinions didn't matter in the discussion. The important thing was for the students to think things through, to figure out where they stood and why. Some time ago, I told a second grade class that I wanted them to try all of the tools in a drawing program and figure out how they worked. I explained that it would help them learn how to figure out new programs and how to use them. Finally, I said that they wouldn't want to call me in forty years to ask how to use something because I would be ninety-seven years old and might not be able to answer. One of the students looked right at me and said, "Oh, Mrs. Jewell, you'll still always answer our questions." One of those LOL moments that makes teaching the most fun!

Despite their faith in their teachers, we're just humans. I try to be the very best role model I can be and I try to help the students learn to use their skills and abilities to really analyze. When students start believing that their teachers know everything and that they need to be like clones, there's a problem. If we believe that someone is so perfect that they should be followed, then we are going to be disappointed. Certainly you can obtain knowledge from someone else and you can get great advice from them. You can get a listening ear to work out the possibilities and someone who cares enough to help with the process. But if you're getting "think this" and "do this" on something that is really your decision to be made, then you are following too closely.

The caveat I would give here is that if you are at an age

where you are still dependent on your parent or parents, then you need to understand that they are doing their job when they are telling you can't take the car out tonight because you have biology and math homework. They are teaching you to prioritize. If your teacher tells you that you cannot play football in the lobby where you can knock over the display case, it is not advice or a suggestion. It's a neon sign that says "THINK!" If you are a working adult and your boss says that the report needs to be on their desk by 8:00 am on Friday morning, they are not adding, "If you think that's okay." A policeman who is ticketing you will not listen to "I don't believe in red lights." There are people in authority and there are rules we need to live by.

The problem is when we begin to think that you need to be exactly like other people because they know everything and you know nothing. You can love these people, trust these people, admire these people—but get them off the pedestal before they fall off and crush you.

Peer pressure is just following a whole group instead of an individual. Generally, that group is being led by an individual, but the pressure comes from the group. It makes it more likely that someone might be following into a course of action they generally wouldn't take. It's great to have a group of friends who aren't forcing you to be someone else. What is not so good to have a group of robots who follow course even if it's heading to the detention center or jail because they all played follow the leader into the stolen car or into a bar where they decided to lose all inhibitions before getting behind the wheel of a car.

Many people follow individuals they don't even know: music idols, actors, sports players, politicians. They may be bright, articulate, thoughtful, caring people. but it may be just the character you see on TV. People turn them into idols and decide to be like them. Then a scandal breaks out and the followers are left hurt. Who are these people that we should be exactly like them? Just people. Some do have much to admire about them. You can admire, but it's idealizing and idolizing that causes the problems for us.

What or who are you following and why?

Years ago, I had a student ask me what year I graduated (I know it's bad taste, but I've never seen any reason to hide my age and still don't—they knew I didn't care if they asked). When I told them 1975, their answer showed an incredibly inaccurate view of history.

"I know what you did."

"Um, what?

"You sat around in bell bottoms and smoked pot."

I assured them that I absolutely, positively sat around in bell bottoms. I just never smoked pot. I never even smoked a regular cigarette. They insisted that I must have because "everyone" did. What a terrible perception of my generation.

"But everyone's doing it" has never been a good excuse. Because you see, not everyone is. Not then, not now. I don't know the exact percent in either my generation or today's. I can tell you that I knew lots of people who did take drugs and many who didn't. Some of my friends smoked, drank, took drugs, and some of my friends didn't. I didn't choose my friends based on every little behavior and I sure didn't choose my behavior based on every friend.

I know some people who have recovered from addiction and alcoholism. They are brave and courageous people who took the difficult steps of getting free. They choose to continue those steps daily.

They have to stop looking at other people to control their behavior.

I know people who have walked away from controlling relationships—whether they were parent/child, or a friend, or a boyfriend/girlfriend, they were in unhealthy relationships. It wasn't easy but they found their voice to stand and say, "No more."

I cannot say that I understand what they've been through, because I have been blessed to be in safe relationships. But I can admire their bravery in deciding that they were no longer going to be controlled by someone else. I can rejoice with them as they taste the joy of freedom from letting a thing or another human being control who they are.

When I was a little girl, I had to walk 9/10 of a mile to school. The girl next door got to ride the bus as her driveway was a little further away—definitely not fair. That notwithstanding, along with the walking habits I mentioned earlier, I also kicked a stone all the way to school (and then hid) and then all the way home before hiding it under a rose bush in my own yard. Needless to say, I could have slept in a little longer without these habits, because it sure would have been a whole lot quicker to just walk.

Even raised not to be superstitious, we humans tend to pick up little fears or worries or ideas or habits to keep us feeling "lucky" or safe.

At some point in those six years of walking to the elementary school, I started thinking this through and decided I'd rather sleep in than keep up the fear. I knew intellectually, of course, that my safety did not depend upon how many steps in each block and whether that rock got to school with me. So I purposely just started walking without looking at the sidewalk or the cracks or the driveways. I just walked. I didn't take the rock along with me. I walked. It felt weird and scary at first. But it felt… FREE. My life did not depend upon the sidewalk cracks. And my mother has never broken her back.

If we are to go below the surface of what is keeping people from real, pure Joy, then we have to dig deeper and discuss all the topics. You can be happy without experiencing deep down incredible Joy. To go there, you have to be able to look at everything holding you back. That may take reflection upon even our pet ideas. The intent is to help break down the barriers that hold us back from the deepest Joy. This isn't meant to be a feel-good, surface-level, funny anecdote to get a few laughs book. The goal is to let go of every hindrance to grasp real and complete Joy that cannot be shaken no matter what difficulty may come our way. So I hope you can hear what's being said here with an understanding that it is meant to help, not harm.

And remember you are free to disagree with me about any point at any time. I am not in control of your beliefs.

That's the whole point isn't it?

• LIFE LESSON 14 •
It's (Not) All About You

Back in the Great Depression, my grandmother prayed for my grandfather to find a job to take care of their young family. Jobs were scarce. At one point all they had in their kitchen was a few potatoes. When a wonderful job came through in Cleveland, they happily left their home and moved closer to start fresh. Grandpa worked loyally for that company for the rest of his working years, raising his oldest two in an eastern suburb of Cleveland and the youngest in Indiana when the company moved him there later in life.

Their son, my father, had plans for when he graduated. He wanted to be a paratrooper. Then polio struck. As he lay ill, the doctor offered my grandmother the newest medications. My father survived and while some survived with serious after effects, he had only one leg a little bit shorter than the other. His life plans altered, he became the first in his family to ever have the opportunity to go to college. With my mother's help and support, he graduated with his education decree to become an incredible teacher.

Dad and Mom raised three of us on that teacher's salary even when times were tough. We'd pick out patterns and colors and Mom would make dresses for my sister and I. I could pick out all my favorite colors of blue and have different dresses than anyone else. Dad would cook Italian one night, Asian the next, and English the next. We'd go to the West Side Market in downtown Cleveland and pick up chicken hearts and unusual delicacies for him to bring home and cook up. I didn't know at the time that these meals weren't expensive. They were varied and delicious.

We would go on adventures. Perhaps it was the wooded trails to hike checking out all the plants and animals. Maybe we would grab the Rapid Transit train downtown to the Terminal Tower and walk around looking at all the shops and stopping at Hough Bakery for a nickel elephant ear. Maybe it was to watch my parents in a Little Theater production when they were doing an old-fashioned (old, old, old-fashioned now, I guess) melodrama.

I don't remember ever feeling like I lacked anything. I had clothes, food, and lots of love. What else did I need?

Sometimes, though, I'd wait for something I wanted. And sometimes, I'd work for something I really wanted.

My sister was going to be a junior at Cleveland State University when I started my freshman year of college. With all of us, including my kid brother, in school, my mom was working during the day, but it was still going to be a stretch to put two kids through at once. So my mom sat me down and discussed it with me in my junior year. If I were to go to a college nearby and live at home like my sister, then they could really take care of a great deal of it. If I were to want to live at a college, then I would need to work for it. Either way, a good scholarship was pretty important.

So I studied, really studied, for the PSAT and SAT. I earned a National Merit semifinalist designation. I applied for scholarships. I went to a couple of schools and took scholarship tests and applied to honors programs with scholarships. I worked part time and set money aside –

even all those pennies I managed to earn waitressing in that brief stint.

You see, I wanted to go away to school. Not because home was awful. It was wonderful. I just wanted to fly. My parents had taught me how to be independent, reliable, and responsible, and I wanted the chance to live it.

Kent State University offered me the chance. Close enough to home to show up on weekends (lots of kids with cars or parents who could share rides) but far enough to be away. It was wonderful. I worked for my grades. I worked in the school cafeteria for extra money. I met new friends and learned new things. I loved it.

One night in the chit chat at a dorm party, a friend and I talked about working for college. They strongly felt that my parents should have just borrowed the money to pay for my education so that I didn't need to work. Nearby, I saw a young man that we both knew fairly well. He had already had lots more to drink than he should have had. But the results weren't an increase in happiness. Instead, he became more morose as the night went on. He was absolutely miserable. I had talked to him earlier in the evening and he had shared how he really didn't want to be in school. He wasn't sure what he wanted to do in life. The course work really didn't excite him. He didn't want to work for it—or anything else. He had never actually worked for anything in his life. The 70's mindset was that his family just needed to provide and push. Their intentions were excellent. The results were that this poor young man had no idea what he wanted to do—he really didn't want to do anything. His life had no real goals, no passion, no idea of future, no joy—and no idea how to get to any of those things. I felt so sorry for him and I hope somewhere along the line all that changed for him.

I asked the friend if he thought that that young man was better off because his parents were trying to push the dream upon him or if I was better off because I was working for my own dream. Working for it, you see, made

it mean so much more to me. I valued my education –
even those classes I really didn't like because I had a goal
and this was the way to get there. I valued it even more
because I was working so hard to get it. It would have
meant nothing if I had walked on campus and half-
heartedly attended a few classes so I could pick up a
diploma without any investment of myself.

My generation was the first generation that had so
many of the population just getting handed everything
without having to work for it. But it wasn't the last.
Although I still see many hard-working and caring students
and adults, I see more than ever before who believe that
they should just get what they want when they want it
because…well they deserve it, don't they?

But I'm not seeing more joyful people. Instant
gratification has replaced hopes and dreams.

There's all sorts of reasons: the changing economy
over the generations, the attitude in the nation of
working—not just to provide for the family as they grow
up but even after they are adults, the changing work
environments and job opportunities, the belief that all
should go to college or start at the top in their fields
whether they want to or not, the increasing technology and
reliance upon it.

It's important to know, however, that the above only
applies to part of the population. We still live in a divided
nation, where too many people are kept down in
segregated areas where there are few opportunities, and
racism and classism are holding people back from
dreaming and following those dreams. We must address
these inequalities and institutionalized racism in our
country and begin to provide the best of education and
options for all people. With this, we must not accuse
people who have been held back of "Not working hard
enough" to achieve. We can and should be working to
make the changes in our society that will end the prejudice
and provide true equal opportunities for all that do not yet

exist. This lesson is not to be used as an excuse to blame those who are held back for not moving forward.

If you enjoy analyzing situations, this topic gives you a lot of food for thought. On a personal note, though, you need to analyze for yourself the reasons that may be keeping you from achieving those dreams that will bring Joy.

That's counter-intuitive to the title of this chapter – but we'll get back there in a moment. Our attitudes about so many things in life are so intertwined that it just doesn't make sense to pretend they're all separate.

So, let's go back to chasing after those hopes and dreams.

First, you have to let go of chasing after all the things that aren't your hopes and dreams long enough to determine what you really want to do in life. What do you really want to do so much that you'll want to keep at it? What do you not only enjoy, but do well and can see as an accomplishment?

What do I want so much that I'm willing to work for it, to fight through the obstacles to get it? What's the cost, not just monetary, and am I willing to pay it?

How do these dreams fit in with other aspects of your life? Do your biggest dreams dovetail with your smaller dreams? Are they career dreams or personal dreams?

Secondly, let go of thinking that anyone should hand everything to you just because you want it. Reality is, that it's worthless to you if you haven't cared enough to work for it yourself whether or not others are helping you along the way. In college, I saw those who did as little as possible or who cheated when they could. In one group in an education class, we each prepared a daily lesson for a unit and then went to teach the lessons each day for four days to an elementary class at a nearby school. Three of us really worked at our lessons, but we saw quickly that we had to help the one group member or their lesson wouldn't get done. We made every effort to help them understand how to create the introductory lesson and what to do with it.

Yet, the day we arrived to start the unit, he stood in front of the class and just stared at them. After a moment, he turned to us and whispered, "What do I do now?" He wanted us to write the lesson and he wanted us to teach the lesson. He wanted the grade but he hadn't learned how to do what needed to be done. In the long run, we all know he wasn't really prepared to teach. I hope he found at some point the career that really worked for him but I hope no classroom of students is facing someone who didn't really want to work for them. In the same vein, who wants to visit a doctor who hasn't bothered to learn the difference between skin cancer and a wart for example? Does anyone want a lawyer who doesn't care if they win or lose the case for you as long as they are paid?

The next hurdle is to let go of any idea that you can't go after the dream because of age, or whatever else you are doing, or fear, or what others think of your dream. You're never too old, you can switch when you want, fear is always something to overcome in life, and it's your dream not theirs. Let go of everything that tells you no.

I choose my doctors very carefully, as I am trusting them with my life. I have had, and still have, many excellent doctors in my life. One of my favorite doctors took care of me for some time, so I was very disappointed when I received a letter that she was leaving the medical profession and that I could choose a new physician from among others at the facility. A couple of years later, I saw her as the mother of one of my students. She had left the medical field to pursue what she loved—art. As much as I missed her as a doctor, I was filled with admiration that she had had the courage to let go of what the world would tell her to keep—to go after what she truly loved and wanted. This was the role model for her wonderful daughter—to go after your dreams. Similarly, I knew an eye doctor who had worked as a professional football player just long enough to get the money for med school. While others are busy pursuing the money and fame of football, his goal was to help people keep their eyesight. I have a friend who is writing the grants and working with foundations to be able to open Bridges Black Heritage Cultural Center in the city of Cleveland. The goal is to create a place that bridges the historical past to the present and to the future, determining ways to bring about Dr. King's dream of a city based upon character not color of skin. We have been watching the dream grow and unfold in amazing ways. She's working in education, another field she loves, while she moves forward, but she's not going to let finances or fear stop her from moving into this next dream.

All dreams come at a cost—time, effort, money. But like education to that young man at school, they don't mean anything to you if they don't cost. And if you aren't willing to pay the cost, then they aren't really your dream. Michael Jordan did not put in 85% of his shots when he was three years old. He spent hours playing basketball to make his dreams come true. He studied the rules and regulations, he learned the plays, he got to know his teammates and developed ways to play with them. My academic challenge team has this Michael Jordan quote on the back of their team shirts, "Talent wins games, but intelligence and team work wins tournaments." No one handed Mr. Jordan his championship ring. He and his teammates earned those rings and my team works together for each trophy they earn. The same is true for LeBron James and the rest of our beloved Cavs when he played with them. I was amazed as I watched them play and cheered them on. And with the rest of my fellow Clevelanders, I appreciated all of the hard work they do not only for the team, but for us—their fans.

So what does this have to do with the title of this lesson? Working hard for a goal is the opposite of asking for it to be handed to you. You are not entitled to having everything you want simply because.

I am not saying that people shouldn't have basic needs met. We should help take care of those in need. People need shelter, clothing, food, medical care, programs to help them with mental issues and addictions. A society that does not help people in need is the most self-centered of all.

Our society is still plenty self-centered despite those organizations that do make a dent in helping people. I'm sure you've heard of the Stanford Marshmallow Experiment where they sat four- and five-year-olds in a room with one marshmallow on the table. They told the children that they could eat the marshmallow if they wanted, but if they waited until the researcher came back in a few minutes they would get a second marshmallow and could eat both. Some gobbled the marshmallow immediately. Some squirmed and thought about, but then succumbed to temptation. Some waited the fifteen minutes for the researcher to come back and took the promised reward. Follow-up studies conducted over years showed that those who waited were the most successful group. They did better on just about every measure. The conclusion? That those who did not drop to instant gratification were better able to work for and wait for their goals in life.

Unfortunately, too many in our society have gotten all that they've asked for and are at the point of believing that they should have both marshmallows whether they waited or not. And they are going to loudly demand the second after gobbling up the first. They are willing to push everyone out of their way who does not see it.

People push and demand and take what they want. They go after the success, the fame, the fortune, the BEST! Life is to be pursued with the goal of gaining all that we want and should have. If others get in the way, then just shove them out of the way. After all, who are they to stop us? You even see this driving down the highways. It's like the old bumper cars at the amusement park—everyone get out of MY way—this is my road!

You don't need more examples. You see this every day. If not in person, then in the news. People who have dedicated their lives to taking from others who are obviously less deserving because they are not important to the person taking. They are in the news because they are now suffering consequences for the way they achieved their success: addictions, depression, bad relationships, tragedy, legal difficulties. Success when it is grasped by those who earned it is a far cry from the "success" of those who have not. The former can bring not only fame, money, relationships, success—but also great happiness. Trying for something we want is not work, it's Joy.

What you aren't seeing in the latter is Joy. You are seeing selfish, greedy, uncaring, unfeeling reality.

Instant gratification is something we as humans show as children, but with caring role models we can grow past it. A sense of entitlement develops for those who do not grow out of it. It's not inevitable and it's not irreversible. It's an attitude and attitudes can be changed. New perspectives can be gained.

Is this an accusatory chapter? It's not meant to be, and not meant to be harsh. It's an observation of a cultural norm that is growing stronger – and hurting many. You see, this is an either/or choice. One can choose to work to reach goals and dreams or choose to whine and demand they be given even if it takes from others. One can choose the "Gimme" attitude and take all that they want in life— or choose Joy.

Choose Joy.

• LIFE LESSON 15 •
"Na-Na-Nanana"

Y ou may be thinking already that I'm going to be telling a story of sometime in my childhood where I got someone, like my sister or brother, and then said, "Na-na-nanana, you can't get me!"

I'm guilty of doing that more than once, but that's not where we are starting here. It's not the childhood attitude that is the concern—it's where it takes you as you grow older.

The last lesson was about demanding what you want. This one is about doing whatever you want. It's about our actions, as opposed to our goals.

My students know that I sometimes motion them to walk on their right down the hall. It's not because I have a compulsive wish to see every rule followed every second. It's because I'm walking in the other direction and I don't want to get run over. Sometimes I ask them to learn how to do this before they get behind the wheel of a car when they're older and I'm trying to drive opposite them. They laugh but we both know I really do want them to learn it before they take out the front end of my car someday.

If a group of friends is going down the hall together, though, they find it much more convenient to walk three in a line to talk, rather than walking single file. So they do. It's the exact same way people act on the sidewalks of the cities. It's not a problem as long as they move over when others are trying to get past them in one direction or the other, just as it's not a problem if the students move over for others.

Yet, walking through the streets can be perilous because people do not always want to move for strangers. Sometimes they don't even want to move for friends.

What about enemies?

This is a tame example. Simply being in someone's way is pretty passive, even if annoying and unnecessary.

What about the real na-na-nanana behavior in our lives? What about the times we are deliberately provoking someone else in situations where we know that they can't "get us back?" In many cases, these are situations where we pride ourselves on how we "showed them" by our cleverness. Our clever remarks or our smart actions that have shown someone up. It's enough to boost our pride and show how much _____ *(fill in the blank with one of the following: smarter, better, nicer, more qualified, funnier, etc.)* we are.

I was once a master of sarcasm. I used it against people I didn't like, those I felt "deserved" it. I used it against people that I had determined were in no position to "get me back" so that I was safe behind my sharp words. Other students, a teacher or two, people I worked with or for, were all likely to hear something at some time.

Between high school and college, as I worked a summer job at a store, I found myself working behind the snack counter by myself on a holiday weekend. Lots of sales = lots of customers. In the 70's without the computerized cash registers, every item had to be keyed into the register and it took a while. It soon became apparent that getting cotton candy, hot dogs, snow cones, lots of beverages, and a variety of other items together, and getting the money and change was going to be a really tough task without the line becoming incredibly long. So I just started taking the money and setting it in piles on the counter behind me to be rung in later. I kept thinking I would get a break in the action, but it wasn't happening. I found myself moving frantically to catch up. I ended up ringing up a whole lot of separate little piles before I went home.

In the midst of the chaos, the assistant manager arrived with a step stool. He stood on it, reached over his head and swiped one finger across the top of the snow cone machine and showed me some dust on his finger. "This needs to be dusted." I looked at my line and then looked at him. I reached behind me and grabbed a cloth, which I handed to him. "Thank you for taking care of that, while I take care of our customers" was not the expected response, but it's the answer I gave him.

And I patted myself on the back. Hard.

I was being rude in return for rude behavior. He was not a manager I got along with or liked. The feeling was mutual. I had won the battle. I just didn't realize that I had lost the war.

The war was with me—not him. It was the war for myself.

I gained satisfaction from my oh-so-smart response. I would have even told you how happy it made me to put him in his place.

I didn't know that joy derived from taking others down isn't really lasting joy. It's a false glow akin to warming yourself in front of a DVD of a fire in the fireplace.

This is true even if the other person is wrong. That manager was wrong. My being wrong didn't have any relationship at all to whether he was right. I'm only responsible for my actions, not his.

I think he felt justified to start it, really. I had not been the most compliant employee. I figured that there were plenty of summer jobs (and there were at the time) and that if he fired me, I would just go elsewhere. I did my job and I was pleasant to all of the customers – maybe not so much to the management. I had already put in work orders for some bad wiring next to the little canal of running water where the ice cream scoop was kept and for a snow cone machine door that was missing four of its six hinges, making it very hard to open and close safely as it had an accordion fold up and down and the weight kept pulling it down. The work orders had resulted in no work. The work got accomplished when I opened the snow cone machine one day and the door came crashing down with the sharp edge slicing through my thigh right above my knee on the way to the floor. The miniskirts of the 70's provided no protection whatsoever. Blood immediately started pouring out and I ran out to tell the head cashier who sent me back to security for first aid. When all the reports were done and the wound bandaged, I returned to duty to find everything getting fixed. I told the head cashier that I would return to my post as soon as I picked up a new pair of nylons and put them on (the quaint 70's also required nylons with those minis). I was informed that I would need to pay for the nylons. In self-righteousness, I grabbed a microphone from under a register and demanded over the intercom that the manager report to the front registers. He quickly arrived startled by the command performance and assured me that the store would pay for the nylons. "Honey, we'll pay for a whole new leg as long as you promise not to sue us" were his exact words. I felt like I had just been handed a weapon. I took the nylons, but I knew that I could now behave pretty much as I wanted with no repercussions. A lawsuit was not even an option I ever considered. I just never said so.

"Na-Na-Nanana."

I'm so glad I wasn't one of those managers who had to put up with me.

Justification for our "get back at them" attitude is so easy. "Well, they shouldn't have…" "Well, if they hadn't…"

But it's like the little kid saying, "They started it."

In my house growing up, that didn't work. All involved were considered equally guilty and were punished. The answer was, "Well, you didn't have to continue it." Two wrongs did not make a right with my parents. Two wrongs were just a greater wrong with shared responsibility.

Should the store have fixed the issues before I got hurt? Yep. Should they have just given me the nylons? Absolutely! Should I have been obnoxious and threatening about it? Nope. In both instances, I could have simply explained what I was thinking without being rude. I could have told the assistant manager that I was sorry, but that I had to continue dispensing food in order to keep the line down for the customers. I could have asked the head cashier to call the manager to discuss it with him nicely.

There are many who will say that this is ridiculous, that there is nothing wrong with letting these people know in no uncertain terms that they are wrong. Those who would have gone a giant step further and cussed them out. Those who will say that the solution proposed in the previous paragraph is just "too nice" and absurd.

"Too nice" is not a term I quite understand. Perhaps if nice were the norm, we'd find a more peaceful society. And a happier one.

Even if people aren't seeing what a change we'd have if everyone treated others more nicely, hopefully those who are seeking a joyful life (hopefully you, if you are now on Life Lesson Fifteen), will find that being in the right in how we treat others is a way to live happily. Proving I could be more obnoxious than someone else never really brought me any lasting Joy in life—it just made me what I disliked in others—and even more so, since I was trying to top them in being rude.

Be careful about claiming that you are better than others. Proving it by being worse reveals your character to everyone. Having been on both sides of this—take my assurance that I am far more joyful when returning "good for evil" than I am getting back at others.

Was this not part of the civil rights movement that changed America? Those like my granddaddy who showed that they were better than their oppressors, not worse and therefore unjustly oppressed. They would have justified the horrible behavior towards them if they had answered every wrong with a wrong. Granddaddy knew how to respond, and his Joy in life was boundless!

Years ago, I was "encouraged" to resign from a teaching position that I loved as they dismantled the gifted program I had been running. The principal who had come to the school that year had some philosophical differences with the program and we had not seen eye to eye. I tried to work out ways to reconcile those differences, but in the spring I found myself in a meeting with several bigwigs where I realized what was about to happen. Surrender was the only option and I took it. I offered to bring in my resignation the following the day and left. I can't tell you it was an easy evening. But after tears and prayers, I typed up my letter. I went into her office first thing in the morning and set it on her desk—offering to help my replacement if they had one by the end of the year and to help with the transition for the students and their parents. I had a letter for parents that explained a "change in direction for the program." The anger had all been worked through the night before, carrying it would have been too much of a burden for me. Sorrow was what she saw on my face, but not anger.

Her response was startling. Her hard look melted away and she began to cry. She stood up and came around the desk to hug me. She apologized. The reality is that we merely had philosophical differences about the right approach to students and to the program. We were able to let it go and finish the year without issue. I saw her again a few years later at the funeral of one of those wonderful students who had passed away in a tragic accident. We were able to grieve for him together. "Nice" helped change the situation and bring back "nice" in return. I don't know exactly how it would have turned out if I had gone in with my mouth blasting, but it would not have been nearly as easy.

The sorrow didn't go away overnight, but it didn't last nearly as long as the anger would have if I had let it take control of me. Or the self-righteousness of my childhood.

There was a choice to make as to how I would respond. By not reacting on the anger or the self-righteousness, or the hurt, I was able to let go and MOVE ON. The Joy was back so much quicker that way.

So I'll save the witty remarks for when I'm having fun with friends and family, and no one takes the Na-na-nanana seriously.

• LIFE LESSON 16 •
Why?

I was warned about that student before he even entered my classroom. He was disruptive and angry. He was exceptionally bright, able to find new ways to twist the teacher and class until nothing effective could happen. He spent most of his time in the office. He was only eleven and he terrorized teachers.

I asked the oddest question when I heard all this. Why? The answers were not a surprise, just a sorrow. There was drugs, there was alcohol, and there was a lack of care that everyone in the school knew existed.

When a student walks into a classroom angry, it isn't just because. There are reasons behind it. Teachers know that when they have students who have angry parents, or absent parents, or parents who simply do not care if the child lives or dies, they have an angry student. There are also students with excellent families who have been hurt by family "friends" without the family even knowing, students who have suffered great loss, or students of angry divorces struggling to deal with it all. For example, those who think that kids who have lost a beloved grandparent should be fine before long do not truly understand the way that loss affects young people, not quite ready to deal with such sorrow. Excellent teachers love those students, show them that someone cares and will give them hope. Students are not computers to input data at rapid rates, they are people. Often, they are people who have been hurt. They must learn that life is worth living before they can learn other lessons that are much more mundane to them at the moment.

This young student was shocked when he first entered my gifted class. I was hired to restart a failing gifted program grades 1-12 in a small local school system. There were only about three classes per grade level and everyone knew everyone. I spent the first month setting up identification procedures and curriculum and schedules. And I learned about the young people who would be in my class. Then I started meeting with the students.

He knew I had been warned and the first class interruption was calculated and swift. I set the class on a task and pulled him out in the hall. I explained that he was stuck with me for the next seven years until he graduated. I let him know that I would be there for him, I would listen to him, I would help him, I would respect him. I told him that he was a valuable person that deserved respect, but that so was I and I expected it in return. I let him know that my classroom was always open for him if he needed help. His angry response was rapid and expected. Why don't you just call my parents like others? There's no point in lying to a child. He knew the truth just as I did. I told him I knew that they didn't really care. I told him I was sorry that they didn't care, but that I couldn't change it for him. He needed to know that it wasn't him—it was their problem. In the meantime, I would be there and I would care. He exploded, "Just kick me out." I laughed and tried again. "No, you don't seem to get it. You're stuck with me for the next seven years. I'm not disappearing, I'm not going anywhere. I'm here and you can't make me leave or abandon you."

We spent the next seven years trying to stave off the

issues, trying to cope and move forward. He was in high school when I saw him slipping into the patterns of home. We spoke and he tried to convince me that it was no big deal. It broke my heart to watch. The teachers, mostly excellent caring teachers, started taking sides as to whether he could or should be helped or left to learn some of life's hard lessons on his own. He left school just short of graduation, as I was being forced out of the position in order to redo the program I had built up over those seven years. I was filled with incredible sorrow.

The good news is that some time later, the young man met a wonderful young women and they married. With her love, he was able to get not only his GED, but also went on to college and post-graduate. He became a loving dad. I like to think that I helped him learn some stability and self-worth in order to be able to live a good life, but it may have been all his wife. I'm just exceptionally glad he's alright.

All of this applies to adults. We see angry people, hurt people, damaged people, depressed people, and it's easy to think, "Get your act together. Brace up. Everyone goes through trouble." And it's true, we do. Not everyone reacts to it the same. Some can bravely move forward with little outcry. That makes it easy to judge someone who is struggling with the pain. However, that doesn't make it right to dehumanize someone by telling them that they have no right to feel bad.

No one has a right to act out against anyone else in his or her anger, of course. The bully in the class is often the angriest or most hurt human. They can't be allowed to bully. However, we can step back and try to see them as hurt humans who need intervention along with consequences. We can ask "Why are people angry, sad, depressed, hurt, or negative?" while still not allowing them to hurt anyone else physically or mentally. There is a cause. We don't always have to find out what it is but we can feel more compassion than judgement by remembering the truth.

Of course, it's really not everyone's business to know the cause of everything for everyone around them. You can't just walk up and say, "Why are you such a jerk to everyone?" But just knowing there is a cause can help. If I know that negative behavior has caused problems, then the solution is positive behavior. The solution is kindness. There is no Joy in being negative to someone because they are negative. Quite the opposite. Caring about others and being kind will not always bring positive results. When it doesn't, you will at least have succeeded in not bringing yourself down in the process of interacting with someone.

Too often in life, we find ourselves reacting to angry, upset people by getting angry and upset. Moods, positive or negative, can be contagious. People are careful around people sneezing and coughing so as not to catch anything. We tend to be less careful about catching their moods. Think about the times that you have spent with people who are overwhelmingly negative and consider how you felt by the time you left them. Then consider whether you carried that feeling with you and infected others. Isn't that the typical human reaction?

Good news is that you can be just as careful about not catching moods as you are with germs. You simply switch the way you are looking at the situation and at the person. Remember that there is a "why?" for them, but it isn't your why and you don't need to react in any way but nicely.

Sometimes your kindness can warm a frozen heart. A miracle can happen, and a person can change before you and because of you.

In that, there is great Joy.

CONCLUSION

I s there a way to conclude the search for Joy? No. Keep looking. Wherever you are in life, whatever is happening, keep looking. Search out others who are seeking Joy to help you on your journey. Don't give up. Keep learning.

Do I believe that there are short sayings that will just make everything alright? Am I blind to either my pain or yours? The question has such an obvious answer.

I do believe that we can learn ways to stay joyful in life and that will make it easier in the times of pain.

Join me online on the Instagram page @patjewellohdajoy and the Facebook page @OhDaJoy to share your lessons in Joy.

All of us are on this journey together.

ABOUT THE AUTHOR

MY NAME IS PAT. Well, technically it's Patricia. I like both my name and my nickname. I'm a wife, mom, daughter, sister, aunt, cousin, friend. I'm a teacher, academic challenge coach, pastor, and writer. Remember though that descriptions are not definitions of who we are as people. We are so much more complex than that. Like all people, I've had times of great blessing and times of great sorrow. This is my life, and I have learned to live in Joy. May you have that gift as well.

ABOUT KHARIS PUBLISHING

Kharis Publishing, an imprint of Kharis Media LLC, is an independent publishing house. The Publisher is focused on acquiring and releasing high impact books, and giving authors a trusted platform to share their stories. Kharis Publishing is also driven by a core passion to establish mini-libraries or resource centers for orphanages in developing countries, so these kids may learn to read, dream, and grow. A portion of proceeds from each book sold goes directly towards equipping these resource centers with books and computers. Every time you publish or purchase a book through Kharis Publishing, your partnership goes a long way, literally, towards giving these kids an amazing opportunity to read, dream, and grow. Learn more at www.kharispublishing.com.

CPSIA information can be obtained
at www.ICGtesting.com
Printed in the USA
LVHW081123281019
635534LV00005B/269/P